Have You Ever Wondered:

—Why nobody at your club wants to play with you?

—Should you have sex the night before a big match?

—How can you beat that blankety-blank who just keeps pushing the ball back—and then defeat that hot-shot who seems so much better than you?

—How a man can make a woman feel good on a tennis court—and vice-versa?

—How to best watch tennis on TV?

—How to play your boss so that you are promoted, not fired?

—What are the best excuses for losing?

—How to know if your club is thriving or decaying?

—About all the other things that standard tennis books never mention but that every real tennis player must know, including the language of tennis (or which came first, the racket or the balls?)

Your time of wondering is over—and a whole new stage of your tennis life has begun when you read—

HOW TO SUCCEED IN TENNIS WITHOUT REALLY TRYING

"If you've ever dreamed of beating players who always seem to win more than you, study this book!"—OAKLAND PRESS

SIGNET Books of Special Interest

HOW TO SUCCEED
IN TENNIS
WITHOUT REALLY
TRYING

*The Easy Tennismanship Way
to Do All the Things No Tennis Pro
Can Teach You*

◦▭◦

by

Shepherd Mead

A SIGNET BOOK

NEW AMERICAN LIBRARY

TIMES MIRROR

Copyright © 1977 by Nouvelles Editions, S.A.

Library of Congress Catalog Card Number: 77-1522

This is an authorized reprint of a hardcover edition published by
David McKay Company, Inc.

(O)

SIGNET TRADEMARK REG. U.S. PAT. OFF. AND FOREIGN COUNTRIES
REGISTERED TRADEMARK—MARCA REGISTRADA
HECHO EN CHICAGO, U.S.A.

SIGNET, SIGNET CLASSICS, MENTOR, PLUME AND MERIDIAN BOOKS
are published by The New American Library, Inc.,
1301 Avenue of the Americas, New York, New York 10019

FIRST SIGNET PRINTING, APRIL, 1978

3 4 5 6 7 8 9

PRINTED IN THE UNITED STATES OF AMERICA

Contents

Him or Her

In all places requiring a pronoun, I've used he or him or his to indicate the human involved. Otherwise I'd have to be writing, "When he or she hits the ball to him or her, then his or her racquet will—" And this becomes ridiculous.

However, in all cases except those that obviously refer to males, consider that I've said "he or she" or "him or her." Virtually everything in the book applies equally to men and women, in this most uni-sex of all sports.

As Billie Jean King (my favorite tennis player of either sex) has said, women can do anything on a tennis court that men can do, and have every bit as much skill. True, everything except take their shirts off.

I probably play more with women than with men because, as a writer, I'm one of the few males in our society who's allowed outdoors weekdays. Tennis skill being equal, I'll take a good-looking woman any day, as either opponent or partner.

Chivalry? Off-court, yes. On-court, no, it has no place in tennis, nor do any of my hard-hitting girls want it, or get it. Nor do they show me the slightest mercy when they get the upper hand, which is often.

Women now play on many any-sex university tennis teams and win matches against men. I even believe they should be allowed to play in men's tournaments if they want to and can qualify. The present men's events should be open to everyone, but there should be separate women's events as well. These should be for women only, and I believe that should even apply to men who have had sex-change operations.

Societies that keep their women off the tennis courts don't know what they're missing. India, Egypt, and Spain, for instance, have had good male players, but I don't remember a single woman at Wimbledon or Forest Hills from any of these countries.

It's Never Too Late to
Succeed in Tennis

Have you read all those books about how to do a topspin backhand and what to do with your continental grip and your American twist, and still aren't really succeeding in tennis? Are you being beaten by players who aren't as good as you are? Are you getting into as many games as you'd like? Do you have a feeling that some players are avoiding you? Do you ever come home from the courts feeling, well, unfulfilled? Would you like to win more matches and, perhaps even more important, to win more tennis friends and have more fun playing?

You can. And the trick of it goes far beyond what your club pro can teach you.

It is possible to make your tennis better in a tennismanship way. It's possible to beat people who are better than you are without cheating. And it's abundantly possible to use tennis to further your ends—your *other* ends, social, financial, and even romantic. It's being done every day.

It's not too late to start, no matter how old you are.

I haven't learned these things from pros. I've learned them in the course dragging a typewriter, a mess of children, and a tennis racquet through nine tennis clubs and several countries.

There are real dangers, you know. Some people in tennis clubs are truly Untouchables. Other players simply don't ask them for a game. You may not be an Untouchable yet. But are you moving in that direction? Be on your guard!

1 / The Untouchables

Every club has outcasts. Are you one of them? Do you wonder why?

In every club there is a caste system based on playing skill, and we'll examine it carefully later. And every club has Untouchables. Does that mean they're at the bottom of the caste system? No, not at all. You'll find some Untouchables in classes A and B as well as in C. In fact some of the people even in lower C are very touchable.

The Untouchables are people nobody wants to play with. They are not necessarily the ones who lose. Many times they are the ones who win—if they can find anyone to go on the court with them.

If you want to succeed at a tennis club and be touchable, remember the first principle of club tennis:

The main object of club tennis—even more important than winning—is to keep the ball in play.

Generally, though not always, the Untouchables are the ones who violate this rule. They come in several shapes:

The Abominable Chopperman

I have seen the Chopperman, often several of him, at every club I've ever joined. He appears in classes A, B, and C, but his natural habitat is most often around the upper half of B. He has never learned how to play tennis, but he has taught himself how to beat the people who do.

His strokes often look like somebody chopping sugar cane, and the ball comes over looking like an egg. When it hits, it starts burrowing underground. He can spin a serve so that it jumps either to the right or to the left, bouncing so low that the only way you can get it up is with a dustpan and brush. If you come to the net, he will do a kind of backspin plop lob that never fails to land exactly on the baseline and die with a sputter. Any ball he can reach with his chopper he can put anywhere on the court, give or take six inches, and no normal rule of anticipation will give you a clue as to where. And if you do get there, it won't help; the ball will have fizzled out like a damp firecracker. The first time you play with him you won't make a single good shot because he'll never give you anything to hit.

So why doesn't he win Wimbledon? Because he has a natural ceiling. With these strokes he can never get any better, and a really good player will beat him by (1) blasting him with a hard, wide serve which is almost impossible to chop, (2) volleying mid-court and smashing those chippitty lobs, and using sheer speed and weight of stroke, especially very wide shots, close to the sidelines. The chopper's fatal weakness is that his strokes are almost all close to his body, giving him little reach on either the forehand or the backhand. He has to be there, all of him, in person. Lesser beings, however, are often beaten 6–0 and feel they've been fighting their way out of a paper bag. Usually they say to themselves, "Never again!" and pray they won't draw him in a tournament.

I've known many Choppermen who were extremely nice fellows, and totally charming and touchable in every other way. They're often apologetic, some even try to learn to play proper tennis, and usually come to the conclusion that it's too late. They are always the Bad Guys at tournaments and are hissed and booed all the way to the final of class B or C, which they usually win.

One especially decent Chopperman (in everything except tennis) never wanted to get into class A. He was content always to win the class B tournament. He used to say, "Well, I'm a sort of natural barrier. If you can beat me, then you're an A player."

There are some Chopperwomen, but not many. The species tends to be almost wholly male.

The Sultan of Swat

The Sultan of Swat is the other extreme. He has contempt for anyone who doesn't hit the ball as hard as he does. He swats everything with all his might, usually hits flat, and has almost no control. He refers to everyone who uses caution of any kind as a "pitty-pat player," and boasts, "I've never played a safe shot in my life!"

His shot is (1) a clean winner, so hard you can't even get to it, or (2) it smacks the net and almost knocks it off the netposts, or (3)—and most often—it is out, far out, sometimes hitting the back netting on the fly. There are no rallies. You make one shot, he creams it one way or the other, and you spend the rest of the time wandering around courts 5, 6, and 7 asking people if they've seen your balls.

The Sultan of Swat rarely hits through the ball; he makes a roundhouse swing that clicks the ball off on a tangent. He rarely uses topspin, and often not even any real attempts at placement. Whether he is A, B, or C depends on his control, meaning his percentages, but he is most likely C. At his best he can be amusing to watch; never is he interesting to play. A good player beats him by simply keeping the ball in play and letting him make the mistakes. An occasional drop shot will drive him crazy.

The Terrible-Tempered Tantrum Thrower

Tennis always makes the Tantrum Thrower angry. You wonder why he wants to play it at all. Sometimes he is angry at his opponent or if he's playing a match, at the linesmen or the umpire, but more likely he's angry at himself. He is trying to show everybody for miles around that he really does play better than this and is in a violent fury at himself for not playing as well as everyone knows he should play. He curses, he screams, he bangs his racquet on the ground, he swats balls into the back fence or into outer space. At first it may seem funny, then it's embarrassing, and finally it's a bore.

The Tantrum Throwers are of all tennis classes, and almost invariably are male. I can't think of a single woman who does it, though there are some, like Virginia Wade, who look as though they are about to explode into smithereens at any second, but rarely if ever do.

A few years ago many international tournaments were cluttered with these angries, and Americans were embarrassed that a high percentage were their own countrymen. I can still name them all, and I'll bet you can, too. The situation is better now. Somebody must have talked to these insufferable brats.

Machiavelli

Machiavelli has studied all the players in the club and knows precisely which balls they don't like. He even keeps notebooks. He will never hit you a ball that you want to hit. If you don't like deep shots to your backhand, you'll never get anything else. If you hate drop shots, you'll get nothing but. He wins a lot, and this is an efficient way to do it. Everybody does it to some extent. Before a tournament match you may confer with your pals.

> *"How do you beat him, Joe?"*
> *"Keep 'em wide, he can't run!"*

Okay, then, use it for tournaments. It's a matter of degree.

And it *is* good for you to play with Machiavelli. He'll make you work on your weaknesses, whether you like it or not. Play him when you feel in a hair-shirt mood. How often is that?

The Poopy Retriever

The Poopy Retriever spends all winter jogging hundreds of miles. He never misses any ball he can get his racquet on, and unless you can hit one at least 100 miles an hour, he can get his racquet on it. The last time he missed a shot was in the early spring of 1967—a bird got in the way. He just poops the ball back with one of his two standard poop shots, backhand and forehand. No matter what you do, no matter where you hit the ball, it will come back, *plop*—soft, uncomplicated, usually not even spun—just *plop,* and slow enough to give him plenty of time to get back to his all-purpose starting position in the middle of the baseline. There is nothing to hit against. You have to make the speed every time, and it isn't easy to put topspin onto a *plop.* Sometimes it's the 23rd *plop* that you hit out, and sometimes it's the 54th. Then you start again, *plop* and *plop.*

When you step on the court with the Poopy Retriever, your friends will say good-bye. His games are called on account of darkness or the early arrival of winter. He is at his best on a slow clay court, and if it's slow enough, his opponent will eventually have to be carried off.

> *"How did you do against Wilmer?"*
> *"Lasted into the second day, then cramps. I'd*

> *worn a six-inch gulley along the baseline, and my*
> *shoes down to the sweat socks."*

Some people try to get him on the volley, but he has an effective passing-plop-lob, just plopped high enough to go over your head.

Nobody can say he doesn't keep the ball in play, if you can call it play.

There's a dangerous variation to poopy retrieving. In fact, it's the best four-syllable formula for How-to-Win-at-Club-Tennis (if you don't care how) that I know. There was a non-athlete at our club, about twenty years older than anybody else in class A. I asked him, "How do you do it, Vic?"

"Oh, simple. *Poop 'em back deep.*"

And the key word is *deep*. Anybody who can consistently hit a soft ball close to, but not over, the baseline can get into class A at most clubs. But you may not always get a game.

There are many women as well as men among the Poopy Retrievers. It's the most common sin among the female Untouchables.

The Line Shrinker

Your close ones are always, but *always* "just out." Sometimes they're not even close ones. Some Line Shrinkers do it deliberately, as a kind of gamesmanship, knowing that one really outrageous call can put you off for the next dozen points.

One subtle variation is to say, "Let's play that one let, shall we? Two balls?" when the call is obviously against him.

Another, when receiving, is to take a first serve that is just out and hit a screaming line-drive on it. If the drive is out, say, "Sorry, Joe, serve was just out." And if your longshot drive is in, and you've made the point: "Great serve, Joe!" Or, if he hits a clean ace, just over the net: "Let! Didn't you hear it, Joe? Two balls!"

All these can help you win, and will also earn you a place among the Untouchables.

Line-shrinking is about equally shared between males and females. The most outrageous case I can think of, off-hand, was a female.

The Ball Miser

One of the biggest regular costs of playing tennis (next to the drinks afterward) is balls, especially if you're playing on a hard court. A quick way to get a place among the Untouchables is to get a reputation as a Ball Miser, someone who always uses the other fellow's balls.

Notable ploys: carrying about three cans, or boxes, full of balls, all as bald as marbles. "Take your pick, boys!" Or, in pressure-can territory (i.e., mostly the U.S., almost never in Europe, where they come in cardboard boxes) bring an unopened can. "Shall we open these?" (The proper answer is "Yes, thanks!") I know people who've carried an unopened can around for a whole season, always getting the reply, "Oh, these are good enough. Bill!" And another miserly ploy is simply "Has anybody got any balls? Left all mine in the car."

2 | How to Be Touchable

You don't have to be an outcast. Try stretching.

ARE YOU A SPOILER OR A STRETCHER?

Nobody's perfect. If there's one player among you, all 30 million Yanks, and all the rest, who has never committed one of the Untouchable sins, step forward. You'll be the first tennis saint, and we'll put a statue of you making a Nice Shot in the niche in the concrete jungle under the Forest Hills stadium, next to the tombstone lists of the old champions.

Nice guys (and nice girls) do sometimes win, and the fact that they get all that extra play (because people ask them) helps their game as well as their quality of life—tennis life, that is.

Orthodox tennis has more future in it; you can keep on getting better every year. But nasty tennis will take you only so far and dump you there—alone, alas, alone.

It's no sin to make drop shots. Deliberate soft-balling is an honorable tactic, on occasion. And as for spin, almost every shot of a great player contains some spin—top, bottom, or either side—if only for control. Remember Bill Tilden's classic remark, "Never make any stroke without imparting a conscious, deliberate, and intentional spin to the ball." ("But *never*," I'd ask the ghost of old Bill, "a flat serve, even as a switch? Never a flat smash or a flat volley?")

Often you'll see two Poopy Retrievers playing together, blissfully happy, running and plopping for hours on end, almost never finishing a set. They're getting marvelous exercise, and who's to say they're wrong? We now even have the tournament equivalent, the Forever Baseliners, like Solomon and Dibbs. People can leave their seats, have a beer, and come back to find the same point going on. The winner is the last man left standing on the court. Is that worse than the three-shot "big game" of serve, return, and volley?

There are even Abominable Choppermen who save their chopping for tournaments and play a "nice game" socially. "The trouble is," one of them told me, "I never win playing nice tennis. Maybe I learned it too late."

DO YOU HAVE TO BE LOVABLE?

Tennis *is* gladiatorial, with death for a week to the loser. How nice should you be? The difference is really a matter of attitude. You do want to win very much, but you want to do it by raising your game higher than your opponent can raise his, not by sabotaging him.

All tennis players can be divided into two categories in this sense: the stretchers and the spoilers. Some players stretch you to your utmost and make you play your best tennis, and others try to make you play your worst tennis. The stretcher is doing his best to beat you, to outmaneuver you, to hit the ball where you're not. He forces you to volley, smash, and lob. He makes you fight and makes you produce better tennis than you thought you could.

The stretcher makes you look good and feel good. The spoiler makes you look bad and feel bad. You're happier coming off the court if you have been stretched into making your best shots, even if you lose, than if you have been forced by a spoiler to play his game, even if you beat him. I feel that way, in any case.

The popular players in any club are the stretchers, not the spoilers, and even when they're beating everybody.

Tennis at its best is, at any level, a kind of rocket-chess, a game of strategy and maneuver as well as running and hitting. The better you are, the higher level you reach, the more interesting and enjoyable it gets. This is why people become tennis addicts. The more you play, the more you want to play.

Probably the best stroke to practice to get into the stretcher class is the topspin drive because it enables you to hit the ball very hard, and still keep it in. The spin helps control the direction, and the topspin (spinning as though rolling forward) makes it pull down, and keeps it from going out. The harder you hit it the harder it spins, and the more it pulls down. The topspin forehand is a natural stroke, and I wish that the backhand were as natural. To me it never has been.

TENNIS ECSTASY

But every shot you make, even in "nice tennis," or stretching tennis, should be a forcing one. You're trying to hit a winner, or starting a shot-gambit that will lead to one.

And one day, with the right opponent, you have that extraordinary experience that can only be described as tennis ecstasy. Like perfect love-making it's a mutual delight that two people share.

For a moment you're both playing way over your heads. At the same instant you're both exactly on your games. You hit your hardest controlled drive to a corner, and he just gets it with his best, almost out of your reach, and it rockets back and forth that way, and there's a topspin lob, and a smash, and a reflex volley on the smash—and finally one of you makes a clean placement, and you both just stand there laughing at each other across the net. And you know then that this is what it's all about, it's why people play tennis. The two of you have done something together that nobody can do alone. You have experienced something that is akin to love, though there's nothing sexual about it. Players, both male and female, with whom you've done this will never be the same to you again, they'll always be special people.

At its highest level, this feeling must be extraordinary. I think, for instance, of the 1975 Paris final between the two young lions (and often doubles partners) Borg and Vilas. They have been hitting balls at each other with such speed and violence it looked like attempted murder. And after the last shot, and Borg had won, they both rushed to the net laughing, and put their arms around each other.

The ultimate success in club tennis is to beat everybody, and win the tournament, having made all your opponents look good, making them all think they've played the best tennis of their lives.

3 / The Caste System in Your Club

And how to preserve and nourish it

TENNIS IS NOT A DEMOCRATIC GAME

Every tennis club is solidly, aristocratically built around a rigid caste system, and the castes are as clearly defined as in the India of the rajahs.

It is as necessary as tennis balls.

The reason is that in tennis you are never hitting your own ball; you are always hitting someone else's, whether it is rocketing, wobbling, spinning, or blooping over the net. And where you hit it depends entirely on somebody else.

THE SEVEN CASTES OF TENNIS

There are at least seven castes, or classes of tennis players, and members of each caste are enough better than the next lower class so that there is no real contest, the upper class member being able to win virtually all the games, or 6–0 in almost every set, with such ease that the game isn't any fun for either player.

This doesn't mean that you can play with only one player in seven; the ratio is closer to one in three. The top three classes account for less than 1 percent of all players. Remember, there are now about 30 million players in the United States alone, and just 1 percent is more than 300,-000 players. The classes are:

1. The very top. These are the players who qualify for tournaments like Wimbledon and Forest Hills. They number a few hundred worldwide—about 128 men and 128 women. On a good day almost any one of them could upset one of the sixteen seeded players. They are virtually full-time vocational players and are the only ones who can support themselves solely by playing (as opposed to teaching) tennis. They follow the tournaments, both pro and open, all around the world, and there's a tournament almost every week all year.

2. The failed qualifiers. These are the players who almost got into the big tournaments, but were put out in the qualifying rounds. They're the kids who haven't quite made the top yet and the recent has-beens who've just slipped off. Some are regional champions. Some appear locally in the opening rounds of the far reaches of the year-long, worldwide tennis circuit. There are several thousand of these. None is able to make a living by playing, but all know that unless they play almost all the time, they'll never make the top class. Many are forced to be tennis bums, trying to follow the tournaments and teaching here and there.

3. The players who normally would be beaten 6–0 by the class 2 players, but would demolish the average club champion 6–0. They're the top 14- and 15-year-old tennis camp kids and the children of teaching pros, and perhaps one in 20 of them will make one of the first two classes. They're resident club pros, some of whom once played serious competitive tennis, and the aging tennis bums in their late 30's or early 40's, perhaps now working for sporting goods companies. They're the better veterans,

over 45. Lots of these older players might take one set from a class 2 player, but would fade in a long match.

4. The class A players of your tennis club, and the top third of the main tennis population. There are about ten million of these players in the United States.

5. The class B players at your club, the middle third, the average tennis players, who take tennis seriously enough to play in every week and have been doing so for at least five years and perhaps for as many as 40.

6. The club class C players, the lowest third of the club match players, the youngest and the oldest, the rabbits, the hackers, the wild hard-hitters, the ones who spend more time in the club bar than on the courts, and the relaxed, who play just for fun and exercise.

7. The beginners who haven't started any match play, the players who've given it up, and the ones who don't play singles at all any more, but like a nice, sociable doubles.

And who decides? You, of course, by playing. There are two major ways of determining class standing, by ladders and by tournaments.

THE LADDER SYSTEM

The ladder system is the most common method of determining class in the United States. It is rarely used in Europe.

Usually a ladder is a series of hooks on a panel (often in a pyramid or triangle shape—usually three triangles) somewhere on an indoor clubhouse wall. There is one hook and one tag for each member, and usually there are three classes, A, B, and C. You rise by challenging and playing people above you on the ladder.

The rules at our Long Island club were simple and fairly typical. You could challenge anyone within about one fourth of your class; for example, in a class B of 40 players you could challenge anyone ten places above you on the ladder. And if you were number 3 in class B, you could challenge any of the bottom seven of class A. If you won, you took the loser's place, and the loser and everybody else who was ahead of you went down one place. Challenges had to be played off within about ten days, and the challenger had to furnish new balls. If you lost, you just stayed in your original place. If you never challenged, the other challenges would gradually push you toward the bottom.

In our club men and women had separate ladders and separate A, B, and C tournaments. There is no reason, however, why classes could not be bisexual, since they are based solely on tennis ability. Bisexual tournaments would follow this automatically. If mixing the sexes would require four or five classes instead of three, so be it.

PLACEMENT BY TOURNAMENT

This system of placement is often used in Europe. If your class isn't known when you join the club, you may start in the club tournament in the lowest class, and if you win, you'll be promoted.

A good system used at our Swiss club is to start the C tournament first and put the semi-finalists from C automatically into the draw of the B tournament, which starts just afterward.

In Switzerland there is a countrywide ladder system. A printed directory lists the names of all club players with their class letter. There are five national classes in the book: A, Promotion, B, C, and D. Roughly speaking, class A corresponds to classes 1 and 2 in my seven-caste list, Promotion to my class 3, and Swiss B, C, and D to my classes 4, 5, and 6. A very good player coming in from another club already has a class letter. If a player comes in from another country, he finds his proper level very quickly. A knowledgable tennis committee member (in any country or any club) can give a pretty accurate class estimate after about five minutes of play.

One advantage of a regional class system like this, with some kind of common standard, is that your club can play team matches against other clubs on several levels. In Switzerland they're called "interclub" matches. You can have B, C, or D teams playing against corresponding teams from other clubs. And there are many big B, C, and D tournaments involving players from dozens of clubs or even players not affiliated with any club. These tournaments are held at a number of clubs at the same time. The top quarter of the draw for the C tournament will be played at one club, the rest of the draw at three other clubs, and the semi-finals and finals played where the largest number of people can watch. Dividing up the tournaments this way means that your club can be one of the hosts to a tournament and still have courts available for the other members. Everyone who runs a club knows that many members would rather play than watch any kind of tournament. But after you've had your own "fix" of a few sets you're willing to watch anything, as long as you can put your feet up and your bottom down.

HANDICAPPING

In England handicapping is more prevalent than a ladder or class system. Though there are many serious competitive players in England, the attitude in clubs, generally speaking, is much less competitive and more sociable than in America. Doubles are played much more often than singles.

Our club in Surrey, a big one, St. George's Hill, had no classes, but there were two main kinds of tournament—one with handicaps and one without. The handicap events were for everybody, and the non-handicaps for the better players, though anyone could enter.

Handicap refers to the number of points given or taken away at the beginning of games. In club tournaments the amount of a handicap can be massive. At our American club years ago my wife was a low A, and I was a middle B, and in our first mixed doubles at our English club we were given a "receive-40" handicap, meaning the score was 40–love in our favor at the beginning of every game played against players with a level rating. Against someone who had a "receive-30" rating, we'd start every game leading 15–love. We quickly got to the finals and almost won that. The next time our handicap was much less, and we didn't do so well. (We were playing on grass for the first time in our lives!)

Massive handicaps are only for internal fun tournaments. In the many big, serious handicap tournaments in England the amount given is rarely more than 15 points per game and is not given every game. If "receive 3-6" is written after your name on the draw sheet, you receive 15 in three games of every six, which means that every other game played against a level-rated player you start 15–love ahead. If your opponent is another "receive 3-6," you play level and start at love–love. If he's a "receive 2-6," you receive one point (your three minus his two) every six games, starting at 15–love only once in six. If you're very good, you may be listed as "owe 3-6," which is just the reverse; in three games out of every six you start with love–15 against you in addition to anything else your opponent may receive. If you neither receive nor owe, you have a "scratch" handicap.

With massive "receives" and "owes" you can have long games. Suppose you are a very good player in a club tournament with an "owe-30" handicap playing a poor player with a "receive-30" rating. You are serving, and the starting score is `owe-30–30. Assuming you win every service point, the score will be: Owe-30–30, owe-15–30, love–30, 15–30, 30–all, 40–30, and game.

In all handicap games you start in the deuce court, as you would normally, even if this means that your score is cock-eyed for the whole game—15–love in the deuce court, deuce in the advantage court, and so on.

Most people find having 15–love against them a big disadvantage, a kind of psychological stumbling block, because losing the first point makes the score 30–love against them right away.

The oddest handicapping system is the sliding handicap, which is used mainly for informal, social, and member-mixing tournaments (see chapter 13). You start level. If you lose the first game, you receive 15–love in the second. If you then win the second, you go back to level in the third. But if you lose the second, even with the 15–love advantage you receive 30–love in the third. The handicap never reaches more than 30–love. If you win the third with your 30–love advantage, you go back to 15–love.

SHOULD I BE A TENNIS SNOB?

If some kind of caste system is necessary at a tennis club, and it is, then is tennis snobbery good?

There is an unwritten social rule in tennis clubs: The poorer player should not ask the better player for a game. Should you, then, refuse to play with people in lower classes? Should you be a tennis snob?

In some cases, yes, it can be a good thing. I know several nice, easy-going young players who have wasted a lot of tennis potential by playing too much in family doubles with Mama and Uncle Freddie and Little Nell. Once in a while for sociability it's all right, but to spend a whole day goofing around with pat-ball players is bad. The rising young boy or girl should play mostly against strong competition and should be stretched and stung into harder practice. The fault in these cases is usually with the family.

But, generally, no to snobbery. You'll find many insufferable tennis snobs in every club, who would rather sit on the terrace all day long than play with anyone a dozen places below them—say, a middle B who wouldn't be caught dead playing with a high C who might even beat him on a good day. It's what he's afraid of.

THE ANTI-SNOB WAY TO IMPROVE YOUR GAME

The snob way to improve your game is to play only with opponents who are better than you are. This is certainly good for your game if you can do it, but all the waiting and sitting will only be good for your conversation.

The anti-snob way is to improve your opponents, if only temporarily, while you're playing with them. One of the best players I knew used this system. He was a top A in the club, usually ranked third or fourth, and sometimes got to the club finals. One reason was that he was always in very good condition. Al was a lean, very tan fellow, late thirties, with a small business that gave him time off on odd afternoons when the club wasn't heavily populated, and the few players who could really stretch him weren't around.

Something like this would happen. Mac shows up, late 40s, a bit plump, used to be a middle A, has lost a lot of speed, now a high B, knows Al can murder him 6–0, but also knows the way Al operates.

> *"Want to hit a few, Al?"*
> *"Sure, Mac."*

Mac is a bit stiff to start. He loses the first couple of games mostly on his own errors, but then he settles down and hits well. He can drive as hard a ball as anyone in the club and has pretty good control. Al is hitting as hard as he can, also with control, and the rallies are good, both fighting to get to the net, good volleys, passing shots, the works, and very evenly matched. They're both dripping wet and having a ball. Mac breaks Al's serve and gets to 5–all.

And then something happens that you may not understand unless you've been watching very closely. Al seems to be hitting at the same speed, but Mac's timing is just a bit off, and he's getting to the ball a fraction of a second too late. Al wins 7–5. They play another set that goes about the same way, and nobody can say that Al has been easing up or giving Mac any points.

Another day Al plays young Johnny, a low A.

Twenty-two, the fastest man on his feet in the club, with a forehand drive like a rocket, Johnny actually looks better than Al in the first eight games to 4—all and feels he's playing the best tennis of his life. Some of Johnny's drives you can hardly *see*. But Al manages to get the last two games, and the second set goes the same way.

In both of these friendly matches Al's opponents had a good game, both felt they were playing over their heads, and were happy for two days. Al had a good workout both times, practiced his strokes, and was in top form for his big match the next Saturday.

What happened? Al would just say, "You can learn a lot from everybody." But what really happened was that Al was playing hard to strength. He knew that Mac could slug it out toe to toe with him *if Mac could get to the ball.* So Al hit hard, but not quite to the edges. When Al hit closer to the lines, as he did toward the end, Mac wasn't fast enough to get there and still have time to make a good stroke.

Johnny was no problem. Hit to his forehand and it was like playing Connors. Johnny's backhand wasn't bad, but he always hit it cross-court, never down the line. If Al ever needed a point, he'd put it deep to Johnny's backhand and come up toward the left. One volley, and that was that. He could beat Johnny 6–0 that way any time.

With everyone it's different, but a shrewd anti-snob can usually get a good game by playing hard to the opponent's strength. And it's very good practice. The name of the game, really, is ball control, and it's just as good accuracy practice to keep the ball almost exactly three feet inside the line as to keep it almost exactly six inches inside. It takes almost as much skill to play to strength as it does to play to weakness.

This can be done tactlessly and even cruelly, making the other player look like a punching bag and feel like a fool. Or it can be done patronizingly. ("Where do you

like 'em, Joe, to your forehand, and not too hard, huh?")
With Al it was never like that. It's a fine line.

Sometimes you'll see a subtle variation of this in the
first rounds of tournaments when a very strong player
wants to be stretched to get into shape. People ask, "But
how could he have lost that first set?" That's how.

You can't get away from castes, and every time you
have a hierarchy, you can't help having some raw edges.
You'll never find a tennis club without a few.

But you wouldn't want a cuddly, blob-shaped club,
would you?

4 / How to Psych Tennis Players

How to beat practically anybody by brain-boggling

If you can't beat 'em with your racquet, brain-boggle 'em.

It is certainly possible to beat people who are better than you are by attacking their minds. It is done every day, sometimes unconsciously, but more often quite deliberately, in every tennis club and in every tournament.

Almost any tennis player would accept this proposition: Tennis is at least 50 percent psychological.

We've all seen it happen to ourselves. We practice that first serve on an empty court hundreds of times to be able to get it in perhaps three out of four times. And then, in that important match we can't get it in one time in three. We know exactly how to hit that forehand drive, and in that last friendly match we put it in consistently. And yet in the tournament we somehow manage to pull our punches and plunk half of them weakly into the net. And then, telling ourselves to stop that and hit out freely, we lose control and start floating them out beyond the baselines.

Why? Was it something somebody else did? Are we being psyched? Can we stop it? Or can we take the offensive and do it to our opponents? Do we want to?

Everyone is vulnerable to mental attack, but some much more so than others, and in different ways, since all minds are different. Tactics can differ greatly. A gambit that can defeat one can actually help another.

THE CASE OF THE TWO FEMALE AUSTRALIAN BRAINS

For an illustration, consider two fine Australian women players, both physically superb, both beautifully coached and trained, and both pleasant and attractive people— Margaret Smith Court and Evonne Goolagong Cawley. Both are more likely to be beaten psychologically than most women players, but in two almost diametrically opposite ways, because to oversimplify, Margaret tends to be too tense and Evonne too relaxed.

The way to destroy a player who is uptight is to create greater tension, and the way to brain-whip a too-relaxed or less mentally concentrated player is to remove pressure, distract, and reduce concentration.

Margaret Court was one of the first women players to be thoroughly trained as an athlete, with road work and weight pulling and exercises in addition to huge amounts of tennis practice. When she arrived at the Wimbledon of 1962, she was probably stronger and in better condition than any woman had ever been before. She hit the ball like a man, probably harder than a woman had ever hit it. The excitement was tremendous. She was almost certain, everyone said, to win the tournament.

I watched her first match, round one, against a very young unseeded doubles specialist. You could see the tension in Margaret's face; she was almost sick with it. Her smaller opponent, bouncy and chatty, didn't seem to be bothered at all, and came whooping gaily to the net to pick off Margaret's nervously-hit ground strokes and volley them into the corners. (They called her Little Miss Moffitt, the chatterbox.) And little Miss M., whose first two names are Billie Jean, knocked Margaret out in the first round. At this time, before Billie had done any serious training, Margaret was a better singles player and proved it the next year when she won Wimbledon. By then, Margaret had learned to calm herself down psychologically.

I don't think it was Billie or her chatting that had psyched Margaret at all. It was the build-up and the tension added to her own nervousness. (Billie, who loved crowds and thrived on tension and excitement, had to train a lot harder, and didn't win the championship until 1966.)

Margaret became more mature and experienced, and seemed to be much tougher mentally in her greatest match with Billie in 1970. Billie had since won three Wimbledons in 1966, 1967, and 1968, and the two met in the best women's match I've ever seen. Margaret, steady as a rock psychologically, beat Billie 14–12, 11–9, in a 2½-hour final.

Was she then psych-proof? Well, not against a real expert, a brain-boggling specialist. The old hustler Bobby Riggs stepped out of ancient history (he'd won Forest Hills in 1939) to prove that an old man could beat the strongest woman in the world almost entirely by brainwhipping.

Bobby admitted it. He was going to psych her. He kept increasing the tension, telling everyone that practically the whole fate of womankind depended on the match. It was more than tennis, Bobby said; it was the male-female conflict of the century. And just before play started, he created a fake crisis over the choice of balls. Because he *had* to have the faster balls, everyone insisted that he have the slower ones, which was what he really wanted. By the time the first shot crossed the net, poor Margaret, in beautiful physical condition as always, was almost out of her mind. Riggs beat her easily.

Was it really true that any man, even an old one, could beat the best woman, or was it pure psyching? Shortly afterward, Billie Jean proved the point. About as close in physical tennis ability to Margaret as anyone could be, Billie couldn't be brain-boggled—at least not that way. She lapped up the razzle-dazzle and the tomfoolery and sent Bobby home crying, thoroughly thrashed. And with only a million dollars to comfort him!

What Riggs did to Margaret was to create an exaggerated sense of occasion, to increase tension, and for most people it's the most potent *whammy* of all. Make the other fellow think his life depends on winning, even if it's only the C tournament at the club.

> *"Well, tomorrow's the big day, Artie, and I know you always play better when it really counts, huh? Me, I'll probably be thinking about our match all night. Sleep well, Artie!"*

You're trying to give him that I-don't-dare-really-hit-it feeling that hysterical illness players call "the arm" or "the elbow," which in this case has nothing to do with the painful tennis elbow. The French call it "the little arm" *(petit bras)*, the arm that pulls its punch.

If you feel this way, yourself, have a brisk warm-up. Hit the ball hard. It's a great time to hit topspin. Tell yourself the harder you hit it the more it's going to pull down.

Exactly the psychological opposite of Margaret Court is the pretty and relaxed Evonne Goolagong Cawley, the Australian girl trained by coach Vic Edwards. She's always a joy to watch because she moves with the grace of a dancer.

And there she was at Wimbledon in 1971, then Evonne Goolagong, strolling out onto the grass, smiling sweetly. "Oh, what a lovely day to play tennis! And how nice! There's my friend, Margaret!"

The only odd thing about her attitude was that there

were some 17,000 people all around and several hundred million more watching television, and it was her first Wimbledon final.

It had been such a nice week, too, and such fun playing Nancy Gunter and Billie Jean, and goodness! Neither one had even won a single set from her! And there was Margaret, looking so frightened. She wondered why. Everybody was being very nice, and certainly no one was going to hurt either one of them. They were just going to play tennis! Mr. Edwards told her she must remember to think about the tennis, most of the time, and she really would try.

And she did try for 45 minutes or so, and the score was 6–4, 6–1 to her, and they were rolling out a green carpet and giving her a great big silver plate!

Her problem was to keep thinking about the tennis. The next year it was such a nice day on the semi-final that she almost forgot about it, and ooops! There was her friend Chrissie Evert, ahead by a whole set and 3–love! Why, three more games and she'd win! She must be having one of those walkabouts that Mr. Edwards kept talking about. So she started to think about the tennis, and right away she won that set and the next one. Wasn't that nice?

The Riggs tactics of tension-building wouldn't have bothered Evonne at all and even might have had the reverse effect of making her think about the tennis. Playing her, the old hustler would probably have come out yawning, and if asked about the balls, might say, "Oh, any old balls, it's not important, is it? You want to warm up, honey, or shall we just start? Nice day, isn't it? Look at those clouds!"

And Evonne later was beaten many times by women who were poorer players, simply because she didn't seem to be concentrating completely.

She's been keeping her mind strictly on business lately.

Her final against Chris Evert in the 1976 Wimbledon was one of the best women's matches of the year, and Chris just squeaked through, 8–6, in the third set.

Things were different, of course, in 1976 at Forest Hills, but that didn't surprise many of us, because Chris hadn't been beaten on clay for three years. She demolished Evonne 6–3, 6–0.

HOW TO PSYCH A GIRL WITH LOVE AND KINDNESS

Brain-boggling can be done by opponents, but it's sometimes done by the public and by the media as a whole. The English have a way of destroying their tennis heroes with kindness and over-expectation.

Take the case of Christine Truman. Six-feet tall, with a forehand like a siege gun, Christine was one of the most powerful women ever to play tennis. Yet she was rather diffident, pretty, and extremely vulnerable psychologically. She was very young when she made her first tournament appearances, and the entire nation embraced her as the Joan of Arc of British tennis. At a time when American tennis stars were lucky to get a paragraph on page 9 of a newspaper in their own country, Christine was all over page 1 in England, with four times as much publicity as the Prime Minister. Every shot she made was discussed on radio and television and was pictured in the Sunday papers. Every time she lost a match the flags flew at half mast. By the time Christine stepped on the court, she'd already been interviewed five times about what she'd do and how she'd win, and afterwards if she didn't, why she didn't. In every game the whole nation was riding on her shoulders, and it's hard to make a shot that way. She often did better away from home. Americans will remember her final at Forest Hills in 1959, when she was beaten by Maria Bueno.

Christine was psyched, lovingly, by a whole nation. She might have been the greatest player of all if they'd only given her a bit of benign neglect. It will be something for Americans to remember, now that tennis has become a mania in the United States as well. This kind of superstar razzle-dazzle idolatry can destroy some players just as effectively as a hustler's brain-whipping.

In fact, most young girls would have been spoiled by the giddy hoop-la showered on Chris Evert when she was 16 and ever after. Her cool, relatively invulnerable temperament has been as important to her success as her fine ground strokes.

ARTHUR AND JIMMY AND THE DOUBLE WHAMMY

Sometimes the brain-boggling is private and very subtle. Take the Ashe–Connors final in the 1975 Wimbledon. Connors was the overwhelming favorite, having beaten Roscoe Tanner in an incredible semi-final that was as fast and hard-hitting a tennis match as I've ever seen. Some of Connors's shots were almost unbelievable, and people were saying that at this point he was simply unbeatable. He would blow Arthur down with sheer speed and power. I certainly thought so.

And no one dreamed that psyching could be used effectively against Connors. We'd seen him in the previous year's final, that quick, almost savage massacre of Rosewall, 6–1, 6–1, 6–4, with not a nerve in his body or at least none that showed. Ashe was the one who had reason to be nervous. True, he'd won the U.S. title, but that was back in 1968. He'd never won Wimbledon, nor had any Black man, and he wanted very much to do it.

So everybody knew that Ashe didn't have a chance. Everybody knew it except Arthur. He thought he had a workable plan. The evening before the final he coolly ambled down to the London Playboy Club, won a few pounds, and was snug in bed shortly after midnight.

Arthur had obviously decided to attack on two fronts, physical and mental. Physically, the plan was shrewd tennis. Don't feed Jimmy hard, flat drives and booming topspins, as Tanner had. That's what he loved. Give him slices, keep the serves wide, and don't hit too much to that murderous two-handed backhand.

So much for the tennis. Arthur talked about that part afterwards. If he talked about the other part, the brain-whipping, I didn't ever hear about it or read about it. But it was there for all to see.

A shrewd tennis psychologist, Arthur knew there was a strong mental strain between them. At that moment Connors had more than a million dollars in legal actions going against Ashe, claiming that Arthur had called him "unpatriotic" because Connors had refused to play for the Davis Cup. (Connors's reasons for not playing were personal and complicated, and he has since played on the Cup team.) Ashe walked out onto the center court grass wearing his Davis Cup jacket.

And in the one-minute breaks between every two games, Arthur sat down, raised his head, closed his eyes, and seemed to go into a trance, sort of an Instant Meditation. He'd done this before, but I'd never seen him do it to this extent. He was absolutely motionless. It looked spooky.

Connors couldn't get going. He looked frantic. He was hitting Arthur's slices into the net and out. Between games he was reaching into his knee-length Boy Scout socks to pull out a letter from his mother. And Mama was sitting in the stands, gesturing, as if to say, "Read that second paragraph again, Jimmy-boy, and remember to hit *through* the ball." Mama was doing hit-through-the-ball gestures, Arthur kept on trancing, and Jimmy kept on worrying.

First set, 6–1 to Ashe! Nobody believed it. Arthur kept on slicing and trancing. Mama kept on hitting through the ball. Jimmy kept on pulling up his socks and worrying. Second set, 6–1 to Ashe—exactly the same scores as last year's first two final sets, 6–1, 6–1, but this time Jimmy had the ones. Five hundred million viewers were amazed. Ashe relaxed for the third set, and Connors won it 7–5. But Arthur was back again, trancing and slicing, and won the fourth 6–4. Once again, the same score as the final set the previous year. And Ashe was the first Black man to be Wimbledon champion. But not the first Black. Althea Gibson had won the women's title in 1957.

I can't remember a more psychologically interesting final anywhere. Certainly there was never one with such a sideshow going on throughout.

It isn't easy to tell how deliberate some of these tactics were. Was Ashe's spooky meditation intended only to soothe his own nerves, which may well have needed something? It certainly didn't soothe Jimmy's.

HOW TO PSYCH WITH A SWEATER

Some tactics that look, from the surface, like gamesmanship, may not be intentional at all. Wilhelm Bungert is a good example. I'm sure that some of his success was the result of a curious kind of brain-boggling, and yet he probably didn't mean it that way.

Bungert would come out on the court looking very cool and even arrogant. I don't say he *was* arrogant. I didn't know him personally, but I'd heard that off the court he was a pleasant fellow.

And Bungert always wore that sweater, a handsome, lightweight wool pullover with a V-neck, even on the hottest days. His opponents were dripping in their short-sleeved cotton Fred Perry and Lacoste tennis shirts, and there was Bungert, his sweater smooth and formal-looking, the neat cuffs down at his wrists, and rarely a hair on his head out of place. He moved as though he were marching on a parade ground. It was said that he could hit a drive standing at attention. His opponents must have wondered if they should salute. It would have driven me out of my mind.

It must have worked. Bungert was a true amateur player, not one of the "shamateurs" of that day who played the tennis circuit every week all year long. He was a sports dealer in Germany and played only a few months in the summer. Yet he reached the Wimbledon final in 1967 and was beaten by Newcombe. It wasn't a fluke, either; he'd done well many times before. In 1963 he knocked out the top seed, Emerson, and was beaten in the semi-finals by another expert brain-boggler, Chuck McKinley.

HOW TO MIX HUSTLE-BUSTLE AND BRAIN-BOGGLE

Chuck McKinley also used brain-whipping by dominance, but his style was entirely different, and it always seemed to me that it was studied and deliberate. Chuck would stand at the service line and beam an almost hypnotic domination rocket across the net, so strong it was tangible, and then he would follow it with some of the busiest hustle-bustle tennis I've ever seen. Chuck ran, bounced, tumbled, and scrambled all over the court. He didn't fall; he'd hit and roll and come up bustling. His opponent must have thought Chuck had him surrounded and mentally whammied at the same time.

His hustle-bustle was very effective. Chuck wasn't even *shaped* like a tennis player—he was round and compact, like a quarterback, but he managed to whammy and bustle his way through the 1963 Wimbledon without losing a single set. This had been done only twice before in Wimbledon history, both times by Americans, Don Budge in 1938 and Tony Trabert in 1955.

THE RACQUET PLOY

The simplest and best-known club ploy for intimidating opponents is the multiple racquet device—carrying half a dozen racquets onto the court. This has no meaning in bigtime tennis, because everybody brings along an armful of racquets. After all, the stars get them free, and the superstars can be paid $25,000 a year or more just to be seen using the free racquets, which accounts for their otherwise unaccountable switching of racquets.

However, in most clubs anything over two racquets can be quite frightening. No need to buy all that lumber; just get half a dozen identical covers—the *best* covers.

> "I could see the guy was really shattered when you walked up with five racquets."
> "Yeah. Well, actually one has a split throat, one is warped, one has broken strings, and one hits kind of

funny. But this one works fine. Actually haven't used anything else for the last two years. Must remember to get it restrung next season."

"Peachy covers, though."

No player goes further on racquetmanship than Pancho Gonzales, who really does use a whole set of them, each of varying string tensions. He shuffles them around every time he changes court, poking and ringing them to find which one suits his mood or the tactical crisis of the moment. He may use one for serving, another for receiving, and perhaps one with much lower tension for a switch to a softer, spinnier tactic. And sometimes I think he switches purely for effect. If it isn't gamesmanship, it works that way.

NEVER LOOK TIRED

Part of intimidation-ploying is to make your opponent think that you're tireless, that he'll never wear you down, and that time is on your side. This is especially effective when you know that he is younger and stronger and that time is really on *his* side.

One successful gamesman I knew created the impression that tennis wasn't really enough exercise, that he used to run the marathon, and that he now had trouble sleeping.

> *"I never really get warmed up till the fifth set, and then it's over before you know it. Too much standing around in tennis."*

C.M., or Jimmy Jones, the former British Davis Cup

player and now a top coach and editor of *Tennis* magazine in London, tells a story about one of his pupils, Angela Buxton, who was Althea Gibson's partner when they won the Wimbledon doubles. During a Caribbean tournament Angela was worried because her next match was against a girl who had beaten her badly the last time they'd played. The competitors were all staying in little beach bungalows, and the morning before the match Angela got up just before she thought her opponent would. She started skipping rope in full view of her opponent's window, trying to look as though she'd been doing it for hours. The other girl looked out, and Angela waved gaily and went on skipping for another two or three minutes—and then beat her that afternoon.

But whatever you do, never *look* tired during a match if you can help it. That will be your opponent's signal to start the war of attrition, drop-shotting and lobbing.

THE ANGRIES ARE THE EASY ONES

The angry players are so easy to psych that it ought to be illegal. Some are so close to exploding that you just have to light the fuse and wait. But it's important to know the nature of the anger and whether it's extroverted or introverted.

Extroverted angries are set off by any kind of real or imagined injustice, especially a few bad line calls. Some unscrupulous opponents will deliberately argue about calls just to set them off.

The introverted type is angry at himself because he isn't playing as well as he thinks he should. What lights his fuse is a series of his own bad shots, and the brain-boggler will try to force these bad shots by making spoiling shots rather than placements. If a sliced blooper to the angry's backhand creates a flubbed shot, then a series of them can build up a towering rage, and his game will go to pieces.

Bob Hewitt, the Aussie-turned-South-African, could get so worked up he could defeat himself and sometimes have the whole gallery, even at proper Wimbledon, shouting at him. Only between points, of course.

But psychology is never simple. Some mild-mannered players don't play their best until they get angry. Anger starts their adrenalin flowing. Dennis Ralston, for instance, has always been the most generous opponent and a really considerate sportsman. He often gives the other player a point if he thinks a line call in his own favor was wrong. Yet he often tries to whip up a kind of artificial anger in himself, scolding himself and telling himself how badly he played that last shot. He frequently seems to be in a really violent rage that seldom has anything to do with what anybody else is doing. Any attempt by a gamesman to make him angrier would probably help him!

If you want to hear how angry players can get, walk around the outer courts at almost any big tournament. There, just a few feet from the players, you may be amazed to hear all the things they say to themselves. Usually they're angrier at themselves than at anyone else.

THE BAD GUYS ARE SMARTER THAN YOU THINK

Almost anything at all that destroys concentration can defeat tennis players. Some of the court clowning that we see so much of now can be brain-boggling, and often is done deliberately to break up concentration.

But it can be a two-edged sword. Ilie Nastase, the wild

Rumanian, does it, I think, for its own sake. He enjoys playing the clown. But he also knows what effect it's having on his opponent's concentration. However, I believe that it often backfires on him and destroys his own.

When you're playing an important match against the cutest player in your club, think of the tactics that Sherwood Stewart used against Nasty in the 1975 Wimbledon. Ilie was prancing around, getting laughs from the big No. 1 Court crowd. Stewart relaxed and let him get on with it, and then he quietly knocked Nastase out of the tournament.

When the life-of-your-club starts performing like a dancing bear to your local audience, turning his racquet into a submachine gun to rat-a-tat the umpire or putting his racquet over his shoulder and marching up and down or waltzing with the pretty girl on the sidelines, just remember he's trying to break up your concentration, and don't let him get away with it. Try to make it break up his.

Don't get angry, because that's what he wants. Remember, tennis is often a test of endurance, and all these shenanigans take energy. Relax. If it looks like quite a production, sit down. Applaud if necessary to keep him going. And then, when he's wound down, get up and do what Stewart did to Nasty. Massacre him, coolly and quietly.

However, just to prove that nothing is ever simple about that wild Rumanian, he apparently decided to be angelic all during the 1976 Wimbledon and got to the final. There, being the perfect gentleman, he was trounced in straight sets by Bjorn Borg. And their meeting, later, at Forest Hills, was almost a carbon copy—Borg again in straight sets, 6–3, 6–3, 6–4. Some old Nasty-watchers, including me, who had seen him wallop Borg decisively (as in the Stockholm Masters), began to wonder. Does Ilie *need* some kind of private war with a linesman or other emotional skirmish to get his juices flowing?

Of course, if you're naturally villainous, you may want to become your club's Bad Guy *for its own sake*. You can even be a nice guy and have a Bad Guy game. And if you are already an Abominable Chopperman or a Poopy Retriever, you can then compound the felony by being a psychological Bad Guy and make quite a name for yourself.

For example, the Colombian Bill Alvarez, known as the Crocodile, was a pleasant fellow off the court, but he was a deliberate super-villainous Bad Guy on the court. His tennis tactics were defensive, and his psychological tactics were offensive. He was a kind of Abominable Retriever who could keep the game going for hours, and this gave him more time for his theatricals.

Bill's toweling-off technique took forever and was as elaborate as a fan dance. He would sip water like an anteater eating ants. He would walk around the back of the court as though he had lost the service line and couldn't find it anywhere. He would put his racquet on the ground and walk back and forth over it, and then talk to it in Spanish, first lovingly, then with curses, and finally sit on it. The crowd always cheered his opponent and applauded every Corcodile error.

Why did he do it? Bill would confess cheerfully that he was a professional Bad Guy. And he became much in demand with the pros. Like the wrestling promoters, they needed a villain, somebody for the Good Guys to beat. Nastase proved this in the 1976 Forest Hills championships—and also proved how schizophrenic tournament management can be. After Ilie's tantrums during his second-round match against Pohmann, he was fined $1,000, yet his ballyhooed as the biggest drawing card of the event. Signs were put up beside the ticket windows saying "Nastase is playing tonight!" And the crowds flocked in.

So bad is good—and what's $1,000? It was subtracted from Nasty's $7,500 prize money, leaving him $6,500 for two weeks' play. And now that tennis is rapidly becoming a kind of traveling vaudeville, I predict there will be a lot more villains. They may even dress up the Bad Guys in monster clothes and give them funny names.

I've never seen this approach consciously used in club tennis, but we all know lots of tennis Bad Guys who think they're Good Guys.

MORE WAYS TO DESTROY CONCENTRATION

One way to destroy concentration is to create self-consciousness. Simple praise can be deadly.

Max Ellmer, many times champion of Switzerland and now probably the world's best tri-lingual club secretary (and my very good friend), tells of the way that old gamesman Jean Borotra, the Bounding Basque, used this technique. Every time he and Max changed courts, the sly old BB would try to psych Max, telling him how well his backhand worked in the last game or what wonderful control he had. It drove Max so crazy that he finally took to changing courts on the other side of the net.

Very specific praise can be poisonous.

> *"Those were fantastic volleys in that last game, Joe. Don't see how you do it. Must be that funny way you hold your elbow."* (This is good even if there is nothing funny about his elbow. He'll be so conscious of it that he'll miss everything he volleys for the next five games.)

Darlene Hard, who was so good she didn't need to use gamesmanship, was famous for some of her ploys. Jimmy Jones claimed she psyched Renée Schuurman, the South African, by saying to her on the eve of their match, "I'd hate to be you tomorrow if I had a forehand like yours." The next day Renée's forehand didn't work so well, and Darlene won.

Jimmy Jones also told of one of his own matches in which his opponent had been passing him at the net. "You know," he said to his opponent, "your passing shot is working so well I can't do a thing against it." After that, of course, it didn't work well at all.

Every player knows that he can have occasional stretches when he can do no wrong, when he's playing much better than usual, when all the shots are going in. More often, of course, it's just the opposite. But what can you do when your opponent in a match settles into one of these magical spells? It takes real tennis exorcising to break it.

This happened to Jim Jones and his partner in a Cup match against Italians, who momentarily couldn't make a mistake, and if not stopped would have won the match.

> *"What can we do?" Jimmy asked.*
> *"Has to be earth-shaking," said his partner. "How about making a winning volley—off the wood?"*

After a couple of tries, Jim got a real, flubbing, howling blooper that caromed off the racquet frame and barely splatted across the net, winning the point. The Italians exploded, the spell was broken, they returned to being ordinary mortals, and the English won the match.

The serve is the most psychologically vulnerable of all shots, perhaps because it's all *you* and you've got plenty of time to worry and let your brain boggle. So naturally it's the shot most easily damaged by praise. After you've been aced a few times, the way to stop it is to say, "Take it easy, Joe. If you make that cannon ball go any faster, I'm dead." This will bring out all his worst impulses and he'll be sure to lean on it even harder, and the balls will all go splatting into the net.

If he says it to you, forget it if you can. And if you can't, switch over to that hard twist for a couple of points.

Jimmy Jones's weirdest tale of tennismanship was the ploy of an East Indian player who had been lobbing with such uncanny accuracy that his opponent was becoming brain-boggled. Every single lob was landing on the baseline. Finally one went out by about four inches. His opponent cheered, thinking the hex was broken. The Indian, looking impassive, pulled a handkerchief from his pocket and held it over his head like a wind-sock. A gentle zephyr blew it ever so slightly toward his opponent. The Indian said nothing, merely nodded, and put the handkerchief back in his pocket. Obviously the lob had blown out. It would not happen again. His opponent knew that any further resistance was useless.

Even with an umpire, the true dastard can use linesmanship to his benefit. One tournament player (who shall here be nameless) is said to have pulled this one. Early in the match she deliberately corrected the umpire. Her opponent's last ball, which he had called out, was, she said, in, even though it was obvious to everyone including her opponent, that the ball was well out.

Several more times she repeated this super-sportsmanship, though never on crucial points, upsetting her opponent who felt she was being over-generous, and wondering if she herself should start doing the same thing, and call out-balls in.

The gameswoman having established an almost unbelievable reputation for saintliness, then began correcting the umpire the other way on crucial points, calling the in-balls out! Her opponent was so shaken, first one way, then the other, that she lost.

And of course there's the lame-duck ploy. It's difficult to tell when this one is real, or merely gamesmanship. In the middle of the match you begin to limp, as though with a cramp, pretending to hide it, and making brave attempts at smiling through pain. You just manage to get to the ball, but it always looks as though you won't the next time.

A game or two of this begins to set up a conflict in your opponent's mind. Obviously, he thinks, I can win easily over a wounded opponent by changing my game, doing more drop shots, pulling him up, then lobbing him back. He does one dink, but nets it because he's thinking more about you, and then he misses a lob for the same reason. He's torn between aggression and pity and is worried about the reaction of the onlookers. Is he really taking unfair advantage of an injured opponent? Finally his game comes apart.

I've said "he," but this ploy seems more effective in women's tennis, and I've seen it (or *think* I've seen it, since you can never be really sure) used mainly by women. Is it because women are nicer and more likely to feel pity? Or is it because they're more devious? Maybe it depends on the woman. However, many say that the old Crocodile, Alvarez, almost certainly used it.

The falling-down ploy is used more often on grass, partly because really nice grass is pleasant and even momentarily relaxing to fall on, whereas some of the red-dust courts will make you look like a recently slaughtered pig. Nothing breaks concentration more than a fallen opponent, or is more likely to make a player take his eyes off the ball. Must be used only when the situation is otherwise hopeless. Say, your lob is much too short, he has an easy sitting-duck smash, and he hasn't missed a smash all day. So start running, and fall—carefully. If he catches you in the corner of his eye, he may miss his first smash of the afternoon.

One odd case of brain-boggling, whether intentional or not, occurred during an indoor match between Billie Jean King and Julie Heldman. In all indoor courts, noises are magnified. A racquet hitting a ball can sound as loud as a gunshot, and even the footsteps of a woman in tennis shoes can sound like a thundering herd.

Billie threw up a lob, and while Julie was getting set for the smash, there were loud stamping noises. Julie was upset by them and missed the smash. She appealed to the umpire, citing the well-known rule that you cannot "interfere" with a player who is making a shot. Did Billie interfere by stamping her feet deliberately to disturb the shot, or was she merely getting into position? Whether deliberate or not, the umpire ruled in Julie's favor. It had been interference.

Anything can interfere. I think one reason Mike Estep was upset in Paris in 1975 by J. K. Andrews (in addition to the fact that Andrews, whom I'd never heard of before, was having an incredible winning streak) was simply tin cans! The only way to drink liquid of any kind at Roland Garros Stadium was to buy soda or beer in tin cans. Hundreds of empty cans littered the concrete steps surrounding the outer courts where people sat. Every time a spectator moved, he inevitably kicked one of the cans, and the din was like a continual anvil chorus. Andrews seemed to be able to stand it, but Estep was going crazy. He began shouting to the audience, "Don't kick the cans!" His concentration shattered, he lost.

And finally, the most daring brain-boggle of all was used by that most daring of all players, Big Bill Tilden. But you have to be as good as Big Bill was to make it work. Instead of playing his opponent's weakness, he'd start out right away to attack his strength, hopefully before it had reached its full power. If the poor fellow was famous for his devastating backhand, Tilden would pound it. And if Tilden succeeded in breaking down his opponent's strength the man's confidence was completely shattered, and he collapsed.

Your main defense against most psychological attack is better concentration. It is possible to improve yours and win the battle of the boggled brains.

5 / How to Concentrate

Instant meditation tricks to beat the brain-bogglers and your own hangups

You can see that most of the tennis mind-boggling and gamesmanship and all the various forms of tennis psyching are meant to do one thing to you—break your concentration. If anybody does that to you, you're finished until you can get it back again. Concentration is about 50 percent of tennis playing.

> *"Why did you lose, Joe?"*
> *"I lost my concentration."*

You hear that every day at every club. You never forget how to swing a tennis racquet, any more than you forget how to ride a bicycle, but you almost always forget to do all the things you always have to do in order to play the best tennis you know how to play.

Everybody who's had even a week or two of lessons from the club pros knows all these things, every tennis player knows them. And yet after playing tennis for 40 years, I still know that every time I play I will neglect at least one of them if I'm not consciously, deliberately, actively bending my brain to it. And I'll bet that three out of four players will say the same thing.

If you neglect just one of these points, your game will go to pieces and won't come back to its normal level until you correct the error. This is true of players at all levels, right up to the top.

You may remember all the points if you're hitting the ball against the training wall. But in a game, scrambling around, you're going to forget some of them. When you're hurried or tired or just plain lazy, your game can break up, and you say "Now how could that happen? I beat Bill 6–3 last week, and today he murdered me. Tennis is the craziest game!"

What usually happens is that you're forgetting one of the simple basics. The ones I forget most frequently, in order, are:

1. Watch the ball long enough

Of course you watch the ball. You have to watch it to hit it. But if you take your eye off it for one tenth of a second, you're going to flub it, because you won't hit it right in the center of the racquet. You must watch it until the racquet actually hits it. Remember that a tennis ball travels from 6 to 16 feet in one *tenth* of a second. A 100-mile-an-hour serve, not unusual for good players, is going 146 feet per second.

Long ago, when I took lessons from old George Seawagen, he said, "Don't just watch the ball, watch the *seams* on the ball." And some people say "Don't hit it until you can read the label on it." Or "Watch the angle," the angle the ball makes when it hits the racquet and when it leaves.

2. Bend your knees

I know you're supposed to bend your knees every time you hit any ball below your waist. Otherwise your racquet head will be pointing down and you'll be hitting "shovel" shots. I know it, but unless I consciously think to do it, I won't.

3. Stay on your toes

We all know you shouldn't play flat-footed, but most people do most of the time. Suzanne Lenglen, the dedicated on-your-toes girl, wrote that she thought staying on your toes was the most important thing in tennis, and she always was up on them. She sometimes went for years without losing a set. (Helen Wills finally beat her.) After reading her advice, I went out to play with someone who'd been walloping me, and I concentrated hard on keeping on my toes from the minute the serve was hit until the point was over. I won easily.

> "Hey, what happened to you?"
> "I got up on my toes."
> "Doesn't everybody?"

Well, not this body. If you aren't doing it, try it, and see what a difference it makes. It will help particularly if your problem is getting to the ball.

4. Make a good backswing

If I don't concentrate hard on a good backswing, I'll slap at the ball. I have to tell myself "All the way back until you hear a *creak!*" You'll never have any power until you get a good backswing. And of course if you're not turning your side to the net on all your ground strokes, it's impossible to get a good backswing with your whole shoulder in it. I know I've read about top players who were improved when a coach "shortened their backswing." If you're so good you can be improved by having it shortened, go to the head of the class.

Follow-through is equally important, but if you're really swinging back and stepping into the ball, you will automatically follow through.

5. Hit through the ball

For years I'd heard this mysterious phrase and never understood what it really meant. It means trying to keep your racquet going in the direction of the shot after the racquet touches the ball, trying to keep the strings in contact with the ball as long as you can. Hitting through the ball gives you more control. The process of putting spin on the ball helps you to hit through, whether it's an under-hit slice or a topspin. You're "holding" the ball longer, which may mean only one fiftieth of a second longer.

The problem of concentration is that you know all these things, everyone does, but you don't remember all of them every time you make every shot, and if you don't do all of them every time your game will fall apart. The best way to remember them all, all of the time, is to let your game continually remind you of them. It will remind you, if you know how to recognize the signs that your concentration is slipping. Here is a checklist:

CHECKLIST OF CONCENTRATION TIP-OFFS

You're mishitting the ball, flubbing it, not hitting it in the center of the racquet. This is an almost sure sign that you are taking your eyes off the ball too soon, before the racquet hits it.

Too many shots are going into the net. Most often this means you're not bending your knees and thus hitting down at the ball.

Your shots are weak and lack power. This is often a tip-off that you're either not turning your side to the net or not getting enough backswing. Probably both, because you'll never get a proper backswing or get your shoulders into the shot if you're belly-to-the-net.

Your shots are too long, often "floating" out. This is most often a tip-off that you're not hitting through the ball and holding your strings on it long enough. Instead you're clicking the ball off on a tangent and not getting enough spin on it.

You're not getting to the ball. Of course this may be partly because you're out of condition and not training enough. However, if you're not getting to it as much as you usually do, then it may mean you're playing flat-footed and not getting up on your toes. It may also mean you're not anticipating well enough where the shot will go, but we'll get into that later.

YOU WANT A MAGIC WORD?
TRY BELTS

Acronyms help some people to remember things. If you're one of them, try this one: BELTS, as in "He certainly *belts* the ball" or the things that hold up your pants. BELTS may hold up your tennis, too—your shorts and your concentration.

B—is for *backswing,* for beautiful, booming, belting drives.

E—is for *eyes,* everlastingly, eagerly on the seams of the ball.

L—is for *legs,* which include knees (bend 'em!) and toes (up on 'em!).

T—is for *through,* to hit through the ball.

S—is for *side,* which you keep toward the net (instead of your belly) on all your ground strokes.

So, every time, in the middle of a match, when your game is coming apart, sit quietly beside the court between games and go into an Arthur Ashe Instant Meditation. (It'll spook your opponent, too. No need to wear a Davis Cup jacket.) Mentally pull up your pants or your skirt, repeat the magic word BELTS, and analyze which of the basics you're not remembering. I promise you this meditation will help. You can regain your concentration in time to win the set.

Also remember that the next time you see a tournament player with a terribly serious face, don't say "What a sourpuss! Doesn't he ever smile?" He almost certainly does, a great deal, off the court. But he knows that while he's on the court, he must concentrate, concentrate every second and never stop concentrating. Such concentration is necessary for the best player and for the worst. It's necessary for you.

SOME SPECIAL MIND-SHRINKING TECHNIQUES

Anything that helps your concentration or gets rid of hobgoblins of any kind will help your tennis. Meditation techniques have helped many people. Transcendental Meditation is said to have improved some players' serves, and I believe it. Tim Gallwey, the "Inner Game" man, and a former Harvard tennis captain, has applied Zen Buddhism to tennis, telling us how to use "effortless effort," how to concentrate without trying to, and how to stop thinking on a tennis court. I believe that will help you, too, if *you* believe it will. A rabbit's foot in your pocket will help if you truly think it will. Serves, especially, respond to all kinds of ju-ju, scientific, quackish, mystic, or pseudo-supernatural because serving is so vulnerable psychologically.

I've heard of two cases in which hypnosis was used, once with Tory Fretz, an American woman player, and once with an English girl, Caroline Yates-Bell, whose father tried it to implant the idea "You have a good service." Neither attempt had noticeable effect, maybe because the girls didn't believe it would.

Sometimes just simple relaxation helps. Take the case of Ray Ruffels in his match with Vitas Gerulaitis in the first round of the 1975 Wimbledon. Gerulaitis was the new American hope, the wonder boy we all wanted to see for the first time, and he was properly beating Ruffels, the big Aussie.

The match seemed to be almost over and Ruffels almost certain to lose when the rains came. Ruffels, mentally writing off the match, found some Aussie pals, had a couple of beers with them, and relaxed completely. The sky cleared, and Ruffels ambled out onto the court, loose as a goose and with nothing to lose. He knocked Gerulaitis out of the tournament, winning the fifth set 6–1!

However, no need to weep for Vitas. In the 1976 Wimbledon he put out Arthur Ashe in the fourth round and gave Ramirez a hard fight in the quarter-finals.

The latest mental ju-ju is vitamin E, which tennis players are gobbling in great quantities and swear has revolutionized their games. I list it as mental, because so far all medical tests indicate it has no detectable physiological effect whatsoever, either pro or con. Do you *believe* it helps you? Have another tablet! It will help you, of course.

DOES IT HELP TO BE INTELLIGENT?

Or should you give up tennis because you happen to be a moron? Or perhaps just a little stupid?

Don't be hasty. Intelligence doesn't hurt, and occasionally in tournaments we do see evidences of strategy that indicate definite brain activity.

However, the records of the British Lawn Tennis Association show that there's very little correlation between IQ and tennis ability. "Quite a scatter," they say, and cite one champion, who shall be nameless, with an IQ of 80, which is pretty close to being mentally retarded, while other champions have had high IQ's. So you see, at least it doesn't hurt to be bright.

Doesn't that check with your club experience? It does with mine. I know lots of good tennis players with first-class minds and lots who move their lips when they read. The latter, the happy idiots, bash their way through tournaments, letting you worry about strategy. If you can blast it into the corners hard enough, who needs strategy? And they sleep well before their important matches. Maybe they're the lucky ones.

I have another theory, too. It's possible that if a player has a one-track mind and keeps tennis on that one track—well, isn't that concentration?

CAN YOU TEST FOR TENNIS APTITUDE?

Or before you decide to set your three-year-old on a Jimmy Connors course, can you make sure the kid has the stuff?

The British are taking firm steps in this direction. They have an elaborate day-long series of aptitude tests to determine which kids are the most likely to succeed. There are written questionnaires, similar to the aptitude tests given by big companies to prospective employees, which indicate, among other things, the child's standing on the introvert–extrovert scale, degree of cooperation with others, and so on. Some of the tests, like the introvert–extrovert one, are valuable because they are helpful in determining what kind of coaching techniques will work best for a particular individual.

There are various dexterity tests. The way a child handles a ball, rolls it, or throws it against a wall reveals quite a lot. (Letting a child handle balls at a very early age is supposedly a good very-first step toward being a tennis champion.)

Another test requires the child to put little dots in many little spaces at great speed; it is timed with stop watches. I took this test, and it proved quite clearly that even if I started now, I'd never be Jimmy Connors.

6 | Never Make Excuses

But how to make it clear that you're really not as bad as that

Let us assume that you have become a master of tennis psychology, both offensive and defensive, and most of the time you're beating people who are really much better than you are. And maybe even smarter.

Nevertheless, once in a while something slips, and you are walloped, massacred, and carried off the court dripping wet, a mental and physical wreck. It happens to me all the time.

What do you do? Everyone knows that the true sportsman never makes excuses. All he is allowed is a word of praise for his opponent, a deprecating chuckle, and a brave smile.

On the other hand, you know that you are really better than *that,* and it is important to make this clear to everyone, including yourself—without, however, actually making excuses.

The basic problem with tennis, especially singles, is that you have no one to blame but yourself. Unlike bridge or shooting craps, there is no element of luck. Tennis, like chess, is a game of skill. And unlike any team sport, you cannot say, even to yourself, "Well, *I* was brilliant today, as always, but wasn't it a pity that the others were all off a bit?"

When you've been annihilated in tennis singles, there it is. You're the only one around, and if you're not careful, you're in serious danger. Any of these things can happen:

1. You may suffer serious psychological wounds.

2. Your whole tennis reputation may crumble.

3. The guy may never want to play with you again.

So, though you must never make excuses, something is going to have to be done. In fact, you really have a three-pronged problem, with (1) public or club opinion generally, (2) your opponent, and (3) yourself.

WHAT WE CAN LEARN FROM THE FRENCH

The French are the international masters of excuse-making. You must understand first that the French consider everything French infinitely superior, even French tennis players. The French, in short, like themselves as much as you like yourself.

In the French championships at the Roland Carros Stadium they assume it must be obvious to everyone that the French players are playing far, far better tennis than anyone else. One has only to look at the French players to see how *magnifique* they are, and the only reason they are annihilated in the early rounds by clumsy foreigners is that—well, the reasons are complicated and must be explained in the broadcasts and in the press.

It is difficult to blame the playing conditions, because the French players are playing on their own courts, with their own linesmen (who do not always see things as others do), and with extraordinarily lucky positions on the draw.

The fault is never that the French players are not superior. Thus, Jauffret was *formidable* and surely would have won, "but unfortunately there was the wind, which put him off his game." One assumes that the wind blew only upon Jauffret and not on the other chap. Or Goven was clearly the stronger player, "but was upset by an unfortunate series of line calls." The other fellow, a foreigner, who surely did not have Monsieur G's sensitivity, was oblivious to the fact that twice as many bad calls had been against him. Or Proisy "had been disturbed by the outrageous behaviour of the crowd"—of the foreigners in the crowd, one presumes. And one must remember "the unusually high temperature in the stadium—"

These excuses are made not by the players themselves, but by the commentators. And the lesson we can learn is that it is all right for someone *else* to make excuses, as long as you don't make them yourself.

You must not only avoid making excuses, but also vehemently deny that there *is* any excuse, except the excellence of your opponent's play.

> *"Why were you beaten so badly yesterday?"*
> *"No excuses! It's just that Joe was playing so well! Brilliant!"*
> *"But surely that plaster cast on your leg—"*
> *"It's nothing, really! Purely precautionary."*

A sling for one's playing arm is also effective, and a good competitor can carry it off with only a limp and a martyred smile.

PRAISE YOUR OPPONENT

If, because of circumstances beyond your control, you have really made yourself seem an absolute idiot on the court, then you risk losing your opponent forever. He may decide you are not worthy of his steel, though of course he will never say so. If you approach him for a return match shortly after your most recent rout, he may stall. "Well, sure, Dave, love to play, but I promised Charlie that this afternoon—" (No good telling him that Charlie is in Chicago.)

You may begin to panic. Will no one play with you but old ladies and children? You have a public relations problem. You are really better than you look.

No excuses. Just get across the point that this is a temporary setback, for obvious reasons, and just wait till next time. "No excuses, Joe, you were fantastic! Who taught you to play so well in the wind?" (This is good even if there was no wind. He will begin to think there must have been one, and he was good in it.)

Or if you've been belting them out into the parking lot, and he's been cutting you to pieces: "Beautiful defensive tennis, Joe! And me just feeding 'em to you!"

Or if you've both been somewhat diminished by the same club orgy the night before: "Absolutely amazing, Joe! Wish I had your terrific tolerance for alcohol. Just wait till I can see across the net!"

Or if he has been drop-shotting and dinking you to death: "I like the way you use your head, Joe. Anybody can beat guys with just drive 'em back. You were *using the whole court!*" (The phrase "using the whole court" is always an effective euphemism for any kind of really dirty tennis. Subjectively, it always applies to anything *you* do. You can always be sure in your own mind that you were using the whole court, whereas the other guy was bamboozling you with a lot of schoolgirl tennis.)

GUARD YOUR MENTAL HEALTH

But of course the main problem is *you,* and the excuses you must make to yourself are very important. Tennis is a psychological jungle littered with warped and battered minds, and anything you can do to prevent these mental wounds is good. *Sauve qui peut,* and women and children not necessarily first.

The most vital excuses, therefore, are those never spoken, those used only as a kind of cotton batting for your tender ego to keep you from breaking racquets, throwing yourself in front of golf carts, and trying to climb up the back netting.

Keep a handy file of them in the back of your head and pull out one, any one, as you are dragged, beaten, off the court.

It was something I ate. I never should have had all that———just before playing.

It was something I didn't eat. I was really weak from hunger. I ran out of gas.

Anybody can win playing like that (or virtue will triumph in the end). My opponent's choppy, defensive, drop-shotty game may win now, but wait until my clean, hard, honest drives start going *in.*

It was just luck (if your opponent's the one who's been hitting the clean, hard drives, and you've been trying to use the whole court). I was playing the percentages, and he was slamming everything, and today they happened to be going in. Wait till next time.

I've been playing too much lately. I'm stale.

I'm out of shape. I haven't been playing enough.

My timing was off. (This is really the excuse for all seasons, the workable, all-purpose excuse that has saved so many tender minds, and it can even be said out loud. No one knows precisely what it means, but no one feels it is something to be terribly ashamed of. It is more like an Act of God or a stroke of fate. You can be blamed for a bad backswing or for not watching the ball, but if your timing is off, it is something vaguely beyond your control. It is like saying "I think my motor needs to be tuned.")

I've been having too much sex lately, and my adrenalin is running low. My aggression-quotient is down.

I haven't been having enough sex. How can anybody concentrate on tennis with that bombshell in the tight T-shirt and no bra on the next court?

It was just on account of my tennis elbow that——. But this is a whole massive subject of its own.

CAN I USE TENNIS ELBOW AS AN EXCUSE? IS THERE REALLY, TRULY, A TENNIS ELBOW?

Is there, really? It's like asking—is there a Santa Claus—really?

Yes, children, there *is* a tennis elbow, but it is not always in your arm. Wherever tennis players play, wherever teeth are gritted, curses muttered under breaths, racquets whacked on *en tout cas,* and balls hit over sycamore trees, it is there.

Yes, there is a tennis elbow. It is a kind of spirit of wounded tennis that finds its way into that tender little place where bends the arm. It can pain you more *after* a shot than during it. It can even come on little cat feet at the memory of a shot—like that blooper on match point on that terrible day. It can come in a thousand ways and be cured by a thousand more, if you want it to be.

Tony Roche's tennis elbow was cured by a medicine man in the Philippines, where they can take out your appendix without breaking the skin. If you don't believe that—well, he went almost directly from the Islands to the semi-finals at Wimbledon.

Tennis elbow can be cured by a smile or a small silver cup with your name on it or by buying a new racquet. People who play with wooden racquets have felt relief after changing to steel, and people who play with steel racquets have been made whole by changing to wood. People who play with pressureless balls have been cured by playing with pressure balls, and vice-versa, by changing from gut to nylon, and from nylon to gut.

Tennis elbow has been cured by a shot of gin at sunset, a toasted marshmallow under a full moon, bubbling cauldrons, smaller vessels clinking with ice, or secret incantations between the sheets. Elastic bandages, copper bracelets, witchcraft, astrology, and a change of socks have all worked.

Don't let anyone tell you there is no such thing as a tennis elbow. It is the ghost of tennis tears, and it will always be there, wherever we can hear the pitty-pat of tennis balls.

Yes, you can use it as an excuse.

Everyone does.

7 / Doubles Is a Different Game

How to win at doubles without being particularly good at singles

The more you know about tennis, the more you realize how different doubles can be from singles. For example:

Item: The strategy of doubles is much more interesting than that of singles, and it should be more interesting to watch. When the doubles begin late in the day at tournaments, the people begin to leave. But in the grandstand or in the other stadium where the two singles players are going into the fifth set, no one moves.

Item: Players in serious doubles championships often laugh. Players in serious singles championships almost never laugh.

Item: Most tennis watchers can remember the names of the last six singles champions, both male and female, of Forest Hills or Wimbledon or both. How many doubles winners of the last six years can you name?

Item: Arthur Ashe would normally be expected to beat the South African Frew McMillan close to 6–0, 6–0 in singles. Yet with equal partners, or changing partners, McMillan, a doubles specialist, would probably beat Ashe.

Item: I enjoy playing doubles much more than singles. I can remember singles matches I played 25 years ago.

I'd have trouble remembering a doubles match I played last year.

Item: In American clubs I played doubles about half the time; in England, where club play is predominantly doubles, perhaps nine tenths of the time; in my Swiss club, where doubles is almost unusual, less than one fifth of the time.

So you can see that doubles is a game surrounded by contradictions and paradox.

THE DIFFERENCE IN A NUTSHELL

The strategic difference between singles and doubles is based on one major fact: in doubles it is almost impossible to score a winning point with a ground-stroke placement; in singles a ground-stroke placement is a frequent winner.

Most points in doubles are won by a volley or smash, a "kill." Since no kill can be made from a low ball, you must try to keep your returns low so your opponents will have to hit up, thereby giving you the kill position hitting down. The basic strategy of doubles is to keep the ball low, make your opponents hit up so you can hit down, and get to the net whenever possible. What makes this interesting is that your opponents will be trying to do exactly the same thing.

To succeed at doubles you have to be good at volleying and smashing. But ground strokes, especially cross-court ones, are necessary, particularly for service returns, and lobs are essential to drive your opponents away from the net. On the other hand, flat drives down the line will be almost useless because they'll be picked off by the net man. You'll use them mostly to keep him honest, to keep him from bouncing over too far to volley your cross-courts.

In every doubles match, you will play four completely different roles every four games: server, receiver, net man, and the receiver's partner. The latter two don't exist in singles at all, and the first two, server and receiver, are quite different from the roles of server and receiver in singles.

1. *As server,* you'll *have* to follow your serve to the net every time, something only Big Game players always do in singles. Stand farther to the side of the baseline, almost to the alley, and perhaps serve a bit softer (to give you time to get up) and usually to the outside corner.

2. *As receiver,* always try to hit a cross-court return, usually not too deep, to the feet of the incoming server. This kind of return is difficult for him to volley, and might make him hit up. Lob occasionally over the net man's head.

3. *As net man,* move as far toward the center as you can, but still be able to cut off the occasional down-the-line shot. Your main strategy is to keep your opponents guessing. Will you bounce all the way over to cut off the cross-court return? You'll have to once in a while, just to make them think you might at any time. Starting to move over while the receiver's racquet is about an arm's length from the ball (and it's too late to change the direction of his shot) will get you there in time, and your moving may make him take his eyes off the ball and miss the shot. Do this only once in a while to keep him guessing.

4. *As the receiver's partner,* start just a step ahead of the service line, but *don't stay there.* It's the worst place to be, because the shots come to your shoe-tops. (On Long Island we used to call this being "in the bucket.") You're there only so that you can go either up or back to join your partner after he's returned the serve.

HOW TO CHOOSE AND HANDLE PARTNERS

The cliché is that the most important piece of doubles strategy is choosing the right partner, and like most clichés it's true. But the right partner also has to choose you.

The most common mistake is to go for the best available singles player. The best doubles player may not be the best singles performer. The question is, how does he play singles? Go for the volleyer, not the baseliner.

And just as important, is he (or she) compatible? Do you get along personally? Remember, the best thing about doubles is that you're not alone. In doubles you have somebody to blame beside yourself, so you have to be careful not to do it—except, of course, privately, to yourself. It's public praise and private blame that keeps doubles partners sane.

When you play singles, you always remember your good shots and forget your bad ones. "What bad ones?" you say. You've forgotten them already.

After a doubles match you remember your good shots and your partner's bad ones. You walk back to the clubhouse together. The poor devil, you think, must feel very bad about all those frightful shots. I'll buy him a drink to make him feel better.

"I'll buy you a drink," he says to you, which proves that he is already beginning to imagine that *you* have made a number of bad shots. Some people cannot face the truth.

You always hope that next week he'll do better. Great guy, there must be *some* way you can help him improve his tennis.

"Maybe some evening next week," he says to you, "we could have a practice session. Might get some of the kinks out of our smashes."

"Our," he said, and odd that he should talk about smashes. That was the one shot he hadn't missed.

HOW TO DEAL WITH THE ABOMINABLE PARTNER-TRAPPER

Some of our best friends will beat you in doubles because they have managed to find better partners.

In fact, every club has its Abominable Partner-Trapper, who always manages to sign up tournament partners who are three times as good as he is. This of course does not apply to you, since there are surely no people in the club who are three times as good as you are. The trick is to start early, before the tournament is posted on the bulletin board. Cut off the best prospect, and drive him into such a conversational corner that it's less embarrassing for him to give in (and sign up) than to get out.

The Abominable Partner-Trapper, however, rarely plays a second tournament with the same trapped partner, unless of course he has other power-levers besides tennis, such as being the trapped partner's employer, customer, or kissin' cousin.

If you see the Partner-Trapper bearing down on *you*, it will at least mean that you have arrived, and you'll have to use fancy footwork to escape. "Oh, Archie, I wish you'd asked me a week ago, boy! I just agreed to play with Jim!" (Then you'd better get right on the phone and ask Jim.)

HOW TO UP-PSYCH PARTNERS

The main problem with partners is that they're people, and you know how many problems you can have with *them*. So, in addition to all those headaches, you've got tennis too.

It isn't enough that your partner has forgotten to watch the ball or bend his knees, you also know that at the moment he's a psychological basket case, he's worrying about his girl, he had a terrible night last night, and he thinks he's got tennis elbow again.

So you tell him "Hey, Buddy-O, bend your damn knees!" And it may solve the problem and get him to hit a couple of good shots, which will drive all his hobgoblins away and bring you glory and happiness ever after (which, in tennis, means you may win the next two games). Or it could be the last straw and make him go absolutely ape, walk off the court, and never play with you again—or even take up golf. That's your problem. He's a human.

So, it might be better to wait till he makes a good shot by mistake, and say:

> *"Historic shot, Joe! Only a genius or Tom Okker could do that without bending his knees."*

"Didn't I?"

"Not wildly."

"Whadda ya know."

Like you, he knows you should bend your knees, and like you, lots of times he forgets to do it. Doesn't everybody? So he might remember to bend them. Or again he might not. But at least you haven't destroyed his brain.

If he has just completely flubbed the last four shots, so you know he can't possibly be watching the ball onto his racquet, then wait till he hits a good one, accidentally, and say, "My trouble today is, I'm not watching the damn ball long enough."

"You and anybody else?"

Generally, however, it's best to keep the mouth entirely shut, except for strategy bulletins about the other guys, like:

"Bill's always hitting your return back cross court.
I'm going to boom over and try to pick it off."

"Okay, I'll cross back and cover you."

In any case, if your partner's nervous, or self-conscious, it's always a good idea to focus his attention away from himself and onto your opponents, like, "Watch how Jim is messing up high forehands. He'll be a sucker for a lob to the corner." Something relevant like that is better than, say, "Look at that double-barrelled blonde in the second row!" You're trying to shift his concentration, not explode it.

Or, if everybody is tired, going into 4—all in the last set: "They look a lot more pooped than we are. Make 'em run!"

Generally, if you ever create the impression you're "riding" your partner, or if you're ever angry with him, the team is finished. Silence, unless you know him very well, and know that a little kidding can help. And if you can make him think you're relaxed, even if you're not, it will help to relax him.

MIXED DOUBLES, OR HOW BEASTLY DO YOU WANT TO BE?

If you enjoy being with the opposite sex as much as I do, then mixed doubles is the most sociable and pleasant of all tennis games, as long as you play it with certain consideration.

A male slob can certainly win against a timid woman by sheer brutality, driving her from the net by slamming balls at her. Good women players don't mind; they simply volley the ball back and win the point. It's one of the reasons why mixed doubles are so popular in England: women there are generally better than men because they play tennis as a school sport, and have coaching, whereas the men waste their youth standing around on cricket fields.

The best club mixed is usually played with women who are a few notches higher on the women's ladder than their partners are on the men's—for example. A women with B men. Then they can really mix it.

In tough men's doubles, when all four players get to the net at the same time in a real fire-fight there are sometimes deliberate anti-personnel shots. After all, if you hit your opponent, you win the point. Aim for the thigh, they say; the reflexes will usually get the racquet there as a shield, but your opponent's position will be too cramped to make a decent shot. Such body shots are all right for a bully-boy game, but not for mixed doubles. Not for me, anyway.

A tennis ball can sting, but rarely injures. Over the years I've had four pairs of glasses broken on my face from short-range smashes mostly and without ill-effect, but I do recommend and have used shatterproofs, either laminated or case-hardened. Some players, like Ashe, wear contacts.

8 / How to Train

Remember, tennis is not like baseball, dominoes, or other sedentary games

CAN TENNIS KILL YOU?

Well, yes, it can, if you're completely out of shape and if you're used to inactive games like golf, checkers, or baseball. You have to remember that tennis is an *active* game. And if you're just starting, you may want to go easy at first.

For example, a 60-year-old grandmother playing family doubles for an hour will do several times as much running and hitting as all six outfielders of two major league baseball teams playing a double-header.

I know this is true because in my youth (before I became active) I used to play baseball. During an exhausting afternoon in right field I would catch (or miss) perhaps four fly balls, each of which involved walking (and occasionally running) at least a dozen steps. Then I would stand at bat for three full minutes and on exceptional days I would run once all the way around all four bases, spending an active playing afternoon of no more than six minutes and 30 seconds. This can be pretty tiring for a child.

Baseball pitchers get quite a bit of exercise, which is why every professional team has half a dozen of them, so that each one can rest for a week or so after every two hours of throwing the ball.

But all this does get them out into the open air.

Would tennis kill baseball players? Well, some it would, if they tried to switch over right away. Some fellows, known as "hitters," make lots of money for hitting the ball two or three times an afternoon, always with the same stroke—a two-handed forehand drive—without any spin or control. Some of them might very well drop dead after 15 minutes of club tennis. They would have hit the ball more during that time than in a whole baseball season.

Yes, tennis can kill you, but on the other hand—

TENNIS CAN SAVE YOUR LIFE

Just a few years ago it was believed, even by doctors, that it was dangerous for men over 40 to get out and run around, as on a tennis court. It would give them heart failure.

The doctors have now done a complete about-face. If you *don't* get out and run around—as on a tennis court—it will kill you. It will give you heart failure.

If you work up to it gradually and then do it regularly, tennis can very well save your life. It will make you healthier, and help you to live longer. Once you get used to the active life, you'll find that regular tennis, several times a week, is a marvelous conditioner for people of almost any age.

The ones who are in danger are the overweight, oversmoked, and underexercised characters who try to make up for a couple of weeks of dining room exercise by playing ten sets of singles on one or two Saturdays a month.

For the average club player who plays for fun, tennis is the most pleasant kind of training, and certainly enough to keep you in good shape. The main thing is to try to get at least one session in the middle of the week. An hour or so on Tuesday and Thursday is ideal, or even once on Wednesday. This is easier in summer than in winter, and you may find it necessary to jog or work out in a gym. Personally, jogging bores me, and I'd rather play tennis anywhere, anyhow—on a hard court in a light rain, or an indoor court, on an inflated "balloon" court—or play squash or platform tennis, or even work out on the training wall. The purists say that squash is too "wristy" because you bend your wrist too much, and I prefer platform tennis, which we'll discuss later. But any of these beats jogging and gyms for me.

However, for the club player who's ambitious and may even want to play tennis seriously, real training is now necessary.

THE TRAINING REVOLUTION

The revolution started in the early 1950's, and it was begun by a man who will probably be considered the biggest name in tennis in the middle 50 years of the 20th century. Never a great star himself (though he did get to the Forest Hills doubles final in 1939), he started a tennis explosion that knocked out the world's biggest tennis power, the United States, and pretty well kept us down for about a decade. And he did it with a handful of kids and, for the first time, real training.

Harry Hopman, the Australian player, sports writer, and coach, changed the whole image of tennis from that of a polite game played mainly by slender young men at country clubs to that of a tough, high-condition sport. He selected a few promising teen-age kids and began training them like prize fighters. They ran five miles every day before breakfast, built up their arms and shoulders with pulleys and weights, and sharpened their reflexes with squash (Hopman wasn't afraid of the "wristiness") and with hours of brutal two-against-one drills, in which a single player was battered from all angles by a barrage of tennis balls from two players on the other side of the net.

It's hard to believe now, when Australians are everywhere, but it's true that no Australian had *ever* won Forest Hills before Hopman's first protégé, Frank Sedgman, won it in 1951. But that was only the beginning. Hopman mounted his first full-scale invasion of Europe and America in 1952 with a team of boys that included Sedgman. Ken McGregor, Lew Hoad, and Ken Rosewall. Hoad and Rosewall were the 17-year-old whiz-kids who won the Forest Hills doubles that first try. I watched it, amazed. The Hopman gang later included Neale Fraser, Mervyn Rose, Ashley Cooper, Roy Emerson, Rod Laver, and many more. And Australia, with a population about the same as New York City's, dominated the tennis tournaments and the Davis Cup for almost 20 years.

Some said that Hopman was a Svengali and a dictator, ruling his kids with iron discipline (he even fined them for bad table manners!), but he built them into the toughest players anyone had ever seen. Hopman also had one of the world's shrewdest tennis brains. As Tony Trabert said when Australia took the Davis Cup from America, "We were beaten by two babies and a fox." The babies were Hoad and Rosewall, and everybody knew the name of the fox. But the babies were hard as nails.

Suddenly tennis lost what was left of its sissy image, and became populated by characters who looked like halfbacks with muscles like middleweight prize fighters. The lackadaisical striplings who used to lounge around the club terraces were being blasted out of tournaments in the first round, thinking they'd been hit by a truck.

This isn't surprising, since a five-set tennis match, even with tie-breakers, can last longer than three hours, which is three times longer than a 15-round prize fight and longer than a marathon run. It's a wonder how tennis got that limp-wrist image in the first place.

At this writing Harry Hopman is alive and well and coaching in Florida. During the summer of 1976, Switzerland was shocked when a 17-year-old boy suddenly popped up and whipped the whole Swiss tennis establishment, becoming the new champion. What had happened? Where had he been? Well, it seems that Heinz Gunthardt had spent some time in Florida, working with a fellow named Hopman. Same one.

And if you've been listening to the musings of your great uncle—"Ah, they don't play tennis the way they used to!"—just look at old newsreels of the legendary heroes of the long-pants and sweeping-dresses age. Note the speed of the ball, the depth of the drives, the sharpness of the volleying (what there was of it), and the actual stroke-making. I'll bet a dozen cans of the best balls that very few of these heroes could even qualify for today's Forest Hills or Wimbledon and that those who could qualify wouldn't reach the second round. A handful, perhaps, would make it—Tilden, Budge, Vines, Perry, Wills, Lenglen—but not many more. And the biggest difference would be conditioning. How many of them did five miles of road work before breakfast?

Today even the best tournament player can be beaten by a lack of conditioning.

THE CASE OF BILLIE JEAN KING

Take the case of Billie Jean, who admits she hates training. (Does anybody really enjoy it?) And from the first she had so much talent she didn't need much of it.

I was standing on the nice green grass of the Queen's Club in London in 1961 and saw two little teen-age girls playing doubles on a back court. I'd never heard of either of them, and hardly anybody else there had, either. They'd bounce down to the net at every opportunity and put the ball away with some really beautiful angled volleys.

"Come and look," I told my wife, "there are two little girls here who are the best female volleyers I've ever seen in my life."

We watched them knock the spots off two famous international women players, whose names I don't even remember now.

"Who are they?"

"The one who's talking all the time is named Moffitt, and that pretty little one is called Hantze."

Two weeks later everybody had heard of Billie Jean and Karen. They were putting away those angled volleys in the center court at Wimbledon. And they won the doubles. The next year Karen won the singles.

But Billie couldn't seem to make it in the singles. With all her talent, she scored lots of big victories, including that first-round defeat of Margaret Court, then the number 1 seed, in 1962. But she couldn't seem to last the long haul of the Wimbledon marathon.

After Margaret wore her down in the 1963 final, she advised Billie to do serious training. Billie put it off for a while, but finally went out to Australia, where the real training was, and worked hard for three months under one of Hopman's pupils, Mervyn Rose. She did the whole brutal routine: the running, the weights, the gym work, and the tough two-against-one drills. Billie said that at first she could only take five minutes of two-against-one drill, and at the end of the three months she could do it for an hour.

A new Billie came back from Australia—the best woman tennis player in the world. She won Wimbledon three times in a row—1966, 1967, and 1968. In 1967 she performed the greatest possible feat of tennis endurance by playing and winning three finals in one day—the mixed (with Owen Davidson), the women's doubles (with Rosie Casals), and the singles, beating Ann Jones. Nobody can ever top that one. (Doris Hart did it once before in 1951.)

One thing about training is that you've got to keep at it, and Billie did, for quite a while, winning Forest Hills in 1971 (ending Chris Evert's first great streak) and her fourth and fifth Wimbledon in 1972 and 1973.

But could training keep an old lady going? Billie seemed to be finished in 1974, not enough workouts and too much of being a Team Tennis and magazine executive. She was beaten by Olga Morozova in the Wimbledon quarterfinals.

She was determined to win once more, and went into hard training for it. She played regular Team Tennis matches, but in addition, as she told Jimmy Jones's *Tennis* tape recorder, she did "a lot of half-court work, running up and back, lobs and drop shots, lobs and drop shots. Then Mona Shallau and I have been using special running exercises which only we do . . . you stand at the baseline, then run up to the net, then backwards, sideways, back to the middle, up, back, then to the right and back, and so on. You do 30 seconds on and 30 seconds off, building up to more and more 30-seconds. When you get to six of those drills, you can survive any physical task."

How did it pay off? It was a tough Wimbledon in 1975, and Billie was playing a lot of girls who were much younger. She decided to save her strength. "I rested as much as I could, and when I practiced, it was only for short spells, but very hard, to keep myself ready; I was ready when I arrived in England because I had been training so hard."

I know these were hard, fast training sessions. I sat beside an outer court about an hour before play one day at Wimbledon watching Billie slam the ball back and forth with Martina Navratilova. Billie was working hard, but also was kidding with a couple of the ball boys who'd come up ahead of time, calling them "darlings." During the excitement I was brained by one of the balls (actually from Martina) that was coming like a bazooka shell. Almost broke my glasses for the fifth time!

Billie gave up everything—dancing, beer, ice cream. "During the fortnight all I did was go to my room, rest, and have room service. That is not the way I like to live, but that is the way that makes me win."

Things went well down to the quarter-finals, when she met her 1974 nemesis, Olga Morozova, and this year the new, trained Billie beat her 6–3, 6–3. Her down-the-line topspin backhands were deadly. The real test was in the semi-finals when she met the reigning champion, Chris Evert. Chris took the first set 6–2, and Billie the second, also 6–2. Then Chris went to 3–0 in the third set, and we all thought that Billie, so much older, was surely finished. But all the training paid off. Still fresh and strong, Billie won the next six games in a row for a place in the final, which turned out to be one of the most one-sided in many years. She trounced the newly-wed Evonne, now Mrs. Cawley, 6–0, 6–1. Evonne said afterward, "I just can't remember anyone ever beating me so absolutely."

The story isn't over yet. Billie, after entering the 1976 Forest Hills in doubles only, watched Chris Evert's almost boring victory march through the singles, losing only 12 games in the whole tournament, no match lasting as long as 60 minutes. The evening after the final, Billie went back on her diet. "No more bagels, no more ice cream," said bagel-and-ice-cream loving Mrs. King, throwing her hat into the singles ring again. Time will tell.

AND THERE WERE SEVERAL MALES, TOO

In men's tennis, with five-set matches, the new iron-man training standards have shut out all but the fittest.

For example, Mark Cox, the British player, might have been an all-time great instead of merely a good tournament player if he'd trained in the Hopman style. I watched him in the very first tennis Open, the British Hard Court Tournament in 1968. He was just out of Cambridge. Strong, intelligent, and very talented, he was one of the amateurs being thrown, for the first time, to the professional wolves. People wondered if the amateurs would get a single game.

Cox amazed the whole tennis world by knocking out Pancho Gonzales in a five-setter and then by annihilating Roy Emerson in three straight sets, allowing Emerson only one game in the first two! But he couldn't keep it up, and he was beaten badly by Laver in the semi-finals. Afterward he never really lived up to that first great promise.

Seven years later, while Rod Laver was training for his big Las Vegas exhibition match with Connors, Rod hired Mark Cox to be his sparring partner for eight days. In a Bud Collins story, Mark admitted, "Five hours a day for eight days! It was a revelation! I never knew you could work so hard at tennis, which is routine for Laver . . . I got quicker, I lost weight. I felt lighter physically and mentally."

The British press howled. Now as he approached tennis middle age, was Cox just discovering what the Aussies had been doing since they were kids?

There are dozens of other cases. I think of Dick Savitt, who possibly could have been the greatest player of them all. He had beautiful strokes and a kind of tennis genius, and he needed only first-class conditioning. When he beat Ken McGregor to win Wimbledon in 1951 at age 26, people thought he might be the reigning champion for many years, but he disappointed us. In one of his last great matches, the Forest Hills final of 1956, Savitt came back after losing two sets to Ken Rosewall to win the third and then the fourth at 10–8. But then the Rosewall-Hopman conditioning showed. Savitt collapsed as Rosewall took the fifth set 6–1.

Probably the most charming and witty tennis magician I've ever seen was the Italian Nicky Pietrangeli. He could do anything at all with a tennis ball, but he couldn't beat the spaghetti. Nicky was always about 20 pounds too fat, and that's a heavy pack to carry through a five-setter. I remember standing by an outside court at Wimbledon when Nicky's opponent threw up a fairly shallow lob. A Rosewall would have scampered back and smashed it. Nicky watched it fly over like a bird, smiled, and said, "Tomorrow!"

CAN TRAINING BRING MY CHILD TO GLORY?

If you've been reading about how little Sissie Somebody at 16 has just won $45,000 in the last three months by playing tennis, or how Jimmy knocked off $600,000 or so last year, or how various other striplings are making more than the president of General Motors, you may be tempted to push your child into a tennis career.

It can be done, but remember that mastering tennis at the highest level is like learning classical ballet or studying to be a violin virtuoso. It may not be that sublime, but it's that difficult, takes about the same time, and makes even more money. And for all these, you have to start very, very young.

Jimmy Connors's mother, a former tournament player and a teaching pro, began Jimmy's tennis education at the age of three, and said that by the time he was five his game was pretty well "put together." That is, by then he'd learned all the strokes.

In fact, if you want a tip-off, watch the two-handed strokes, like the Connors and Evert backhands. Almost all pros argue that it's better to stroke one-handed, but these kids were so little they *had* to use two hands to swing the racquet—and then kept at it.

The Everts, the Richeys, the Seewagens, the Tee-guardens, the Mottrams, and the Borgs are all families of tennis professionals, and most of the kids were playing not long after they learned to walk. Supposedly Bjorn Borg had never been beaten by anyone younger than himself when he played his first Davis Cup match for Sweden at age 15. Chris Evert almost won Forest Hills at 16. Connors was national intercollegiate champion when he was still a freshman.

You can be sure that right now thousands of hungry kids, hundreds of them the children of teaching pros, are practicing four, five, and even six hours a day. And once they are 17 or 18 and start playing the international circuit (the only places where they can get any competition) with a new tournament almost every week in a different part of the world, there's going to be no time for college.

So, if you want them to get into this business, serious training, including months of expert professional coaching, has to begin before age 12, and if there hasn't been at least statewide recognition, like winning a regional tournament, by about 16, it's probably too late. So let them learn to read and write.

It's a big, tough business now, like prize fighting, and deadly serious. I can't remember ever seeing Cliff Richey or his sister Nancy smile on a tennis court, though neither is humorless off the court. (Any tennis levity is labelled "giggle tennis" by the stern Richeys.) Both have spent virtually their entire lives playing, practicing, or training. Already in England there are reports that ambitious parents, smelling the huge possible monetary rewards, are becoming pushy, and even a bit ugly. That sort of thing is no doubt beginning everywhere, with parents acting like those horrible stage mothers, pushing and conniving.

Do you want to get into that? It's better, I think, to keep tennis for exercise and joy. But mamas ambitious for sons and daughters in other fields will discover that being able to play very good (but not necessarily professional-quality) tennis can open lots of doors—a subject we'll discuss in chapter 15.

DOES TENNIS BUILD CHARACTER?

I don't think many of us want our children to be full-time tennis players, but I think we'd all like them to be good at some sport, like tennis, that they can enjoy all their lives. I certainly wish I'd been taught tennis in school instead of all the useless coaching I had in everything else. Never since I left school have I played baseball, basketball, soccer, or football, and I've always wished that instead of any one or two of these wasted skills I'd been taught a sport I could use in later life.

They say that team sports build character, and I'm sure that my fine character must be the result of spending every spring standing more or less motionless in right field and every fall knowing that on play number 17 I was supposed to surge forward two feet and block out the opposing right tackle. Any original ideas I might have had on this subject were strictly forbidden. I knew what I was supposed to do on all the other 16 plays, too. It is knowledge I seldom use today.

It must have been character I was building, because I wasn't building muscles or having any fun. And I still envy those lucky fellows who were allowed to learn something permanently useful, like tennis, for at least one season of the year. They beat me regularly.

The equipment for tennis isn't expensive, and on most weekday afternoons tennis courts are available in most towns. Twenty kids playing tennis don't need any more supervision and don't take up any more room than 20 kids doing anything else. And when they grow up, they'll have something to show for it.

BEWARE OF BRITISH CHILDREN

On rainy winter afternoons I used to telephone the Queens Club in London and ask their match secretary if she could find me a game. Incidentally, Bea Walters (now Mrs. Seal) was not only the world's best match secretary, but also the nonplaying captain of the British Wightman Cup team at the time, and she knew her way around tennis courts.

"Yes," she said that day, as always, "I'll find somebody for you."

I drove in from Surrey and was told my opponent was waiting on covered court 3. I walked in through the rabbitwarren of passageways between ancient, dirty brick buildings (the nether regions of the Queens Club look like something out of Dickens) to court 3. Nobody was there except a little boy of about 13, not much more than half my height.

"Are you Mr. Mead?" he said.

"Yes."

"Mrs. Walters said I was supposed to play with you."

I guessed that even Bea Walters could make one mistake. I leaned over the little fellow and said, "Do you know how to play tennis?"

"Yes, a little."

"Well, let's try a set then." I hoped I wouldn't make him cry. I hit a nice, easy poop shot to his forehand. He stepped into the ball, and I heard an explosion. A topspin drive came hurtling over like a rifle bullet, skidded across the painted-wood baseline, and crashed into the back wall, untouched by me.

The score was 6–2, 6–1, and he had all the sixes. When I walked out, Mrs. Walters said with a twinkle, "Sorry I couldn't find anyone your size."

"You have any more little kids like that?"

"Quite a few. He's one of the LTA juniors. Training program, you know."

It's hard to recognize my little friend at Wimbledon now, because he's grown a beard. (They grow them very young now.) He's a lot better, too. His name is Paish, John. His father was a Davis Cup player, and now of course he's one himself.

I had several other such encounters with little kids at Queens, all of them on the training program. My ego will never be the same. You can see the bruises on it to this day.

HOW TO BECOME A MIDDLE-AGED TENNIS HERO

It's possible to become a tennis hero even in advanced middle age. And you don't have to win a single match.

My own favorite tennis heroes are a woman and a Black man, and they both became heroes at an age when all the lesser heroes could beat them. The man: Dr. Walter Johnson, general practitioner, of Lynchburg, Virginia; the woman, Jean Hoxie, of Hamtramck, Michigan.

Both loved tennis and kids, and unlike Hopman, who had the pick of Australia's best juniors, Johnson and Hoxie gathered up ethnic ghetto kids, most of them poor and from families who'd scarcely heard about tennis. When necessary they furnished racquets, balls, rides, and even food.

Before Dr. Johnson, nobody had ever heard of a top-flight Black tennis player. He decided to change that. He had his own court and started coaching young Blacks. Because there weren't enough racquets for everybody, he started them off with broomsticks cut to racquet length. Try that sometime if you're having trouble hitting the ball with the center of your racquet.

The doctor taught them tennis, and more than that he encouraged them to be ladies and gentlemen. Everybody knows his two star pupils, Althea Gibson and Arthur Ashe, both of them champions of Wimbledon, Forest Hills, and just about everywhere else.

Jean Hoxie's kids were Slavic-Americans who lived in Hamtramck, Michigan, near Detroit. Most of their parents worked on the car assembly lines. Few of the kids had ever held a racquet in their hands. Mrs. Hoxie started them off with practice against the wall of the school gym. Then they took turns on the one tennis court.

When they were good enough, she took them in her car first to local tournaments and then to Michigan state championships. Finally she sent them on to national junior championships, many of which they won. Two of her better known pupils are Fred Kovaleski, who had many victories at Forest Hills and Wimbledon, and Jane "Peaches" Bartkowicz, a junior champion who played on the U.S. Wightman Cup team. Mrs. Hoxie herself won the Coach of the Year award and was Woman of the Year in 1952.

There have been many other middle-aged tennis heroes who have been better known for their coaching than their playing. One who was known for both was Hazel Wightman, whose career was so long she seemed to be two people: the Hazel Hotchkiss tennis champion of 1909 and often thereafter, and the Hazel Wightman who became the "grandmother of American tennis"—coach, advisor, helper, and friend to dozens of women players, and donor of the Wightman Cup. She coached Helen Wills and Helen Jacobs in the 1920's and continued coaching all the way into the 1970's.

Eleanor "Teach" Tennant made the first ten, but is better known as a coach, first of Alice Marble and then of Maureen "Little Mo" Connolly. And there are many others.

Almost every town and every club has a middle-aged tennis hero who is more interested in bringing along the kids than another silver cup.

THE GODPARENT SYSTEM

One way to begin helping the kids is to start a "godparent system" at your club. Or if you already have one, to join it. Our Swiss club has one, and it works well. Our kids do better in the local junior events than those from any other club.

Each ambitious child who wants to train and improve is assigned to a "godfather" or "godmother" (one godchild per godparent), one of the better players in the club, who coaches and plays with the child.

This system is especially helpful to young players whose parents or brothers or sisters don't play tennis. It is a good supplement to professional coaching but shouldn't replace it. All young players should be taught from the beginning how to do the basic strokes.

WHEN AM I TOO OLD TO PLAY TENNIS?

People ask me this as though tennis were a game for children, like hopscotch or leapfrog, that you have to stop playing when you reach the age of reason.

This is nonsense. Tennis is like sex. If you keep at it

and stay in good shape, you can enjoy it as much at 70 or even 80. You just won't want to do quite as much of it, but you'll feel marvelous if you do just enough. Some think it's a good idea to switch to doubles after 70. I'm talking about tennis. With sex you can keep right on with singles.

Players from many of my clubs have, at the age of 60, and even 70, walloped young lions of 20. And some people don't even take up tennis until late middle age or even old age. Consider Sir David Brown, for instance, the man who built the Aston Martin sport cars. (The DB mark initials stand for David Brown.) Brown took up tennis in his 60's, and won a local doubles tournament when he was over 70.

Many professionals have played well beyond middle age. Hazel Wightman won the U.S. women's indoor doubles in 1943 at the age of 57, and at 64 she won the women's veteran doubles, which is open to all women over 40. Jean Borotra, who won Wimbledon in 1924 and 1926, was *still* playing in the 1976 championships at the age of 78 in the veteran doubles! He was playing well enough to give club champions a very rough time indeed.

Tennis magazine recently reported the findings of Dr. Daniel Kellund, an orthopedic surgeon at the University of Virginia Hospital. He filmed, interviewed, and physically examined 28 players in a super senior tournament, age 70 and over. Dr. Kellund said, "The ordinary old person has high blood pressure, varicose veins, and swelling of the legs, but these players don't. It's as if their whole system is flushed out by the activity."

THE MEAD TENNIS-STOPPING FORMULA

I find, at 63, that it now takes me a bit longer to warm up, to get rid of the stiffness. What used to take 10 minutes may now take 20. And I also find that after several sets of singles I begin to slow down. The time of warming up seems to increase slightly over the years, and the slowing down seems to come progressively a bit more quickly.

The Mead Formula for Tennis-Stopping is: When the time it takes you to warm up reaches the time it takes you to be too tired to play, then stop. Or to put it mathematically, when "f" (time it takes to become fatigued) minus "w" (time it takes to warm up) equals zero, or

$$f - w = 0$$

then take up a game like golf or dominoes that you can play sitting down.

My calculations lead me to believe this should occur at approximately the age of 80. Perhaps by then they'll have invented the tennis cart.

A WORKING CITIZEN'S TRAINING PROGRAM

Let's admit that tennis at its highest level is a full-time job. And also that at its lowest level it's a lot of fun, and if you play it several times a week, it's all the training you need to keep from going to pot. Forget all that miserable jogging and have a ball.

But if you're in the middle ground and want to rise on the club ladder or be the local champion, a certain amount of sweatsock work is necessary, especially on those days when you don't play.

1. Weekends

If you're the normal club player, you'll have all the exercise you need on weekends. You may want to do some loosening-up calisthenics in the morning, but nothing else.

2. Mondays

If you've really played hard both Saturday and Sunday, Monday can be a day of physical rest. And try not to go to sleep in the office. Do calisthenics, and if you have a wall handy, hit a few hundred shots for 15 or 20 minutes, concentrating on those that gave you trouble over the weekend.

3. Other days when you don't play

Run at least two miles, or jog half an hour. Spend half an hour either on the wall or serving with a bucket of balls. Two sessions a week on the wall and one session a week of serving will improve your game almost beyond belief.

On the other hand, if you're young and really ambitious, and want to make your school's tennis team or get a tennis scholarship to a good university, you'll want to work harder.

THE HARD-AS-NAILS TENNIS TEAM TRAINING PROGRAM FOR THE YOUNG ATHLETE

1. Running

Run at least three miles every day, even when you're playing (though not when you're playing tournament matches).

2. Practice

Half an hour on the wall, or bucket-of-balls serving, or stroke practice with a friend every day.

3. Exercises

Twenty minutes of calisthenics every day.

4. Playing

At least two hours every day.

Conscientious training will show in your big matches. When you go into the final set and see your opponent beginning to look tired, you'll feel good. You'll know then that you've got him and you're going to win.

9/Training Aids

Very little equipment can take you a long way

My favorite training device is a beautiful day, a good court, and one of my hard-hitting pals, male or female, on the other side of the net. Heaven is only as far away as that.

But sometimes you need artificial substitutes.

THE WALL, THE WALL, THE TERRIBLE WALL

Every tennis club must have a practice wall and preferably two or three. The wall is the punching bag of tennis players, the indispensable training aid, and the only kind of tennis where you have absolutely no one to blame but yourself. This is probably why so many players, especially beginners, hate the wall. It just gives you back what you give it—no compromises, no excuses.

Every player who wants to improve should have access to some kind of wall that's available every day. If the club is just down the street, go there. If not, fix up something—the back of the garage, the side of the house, even the inside of an empty garage.

Ideally the surface of the wall is tilted back a bit, the top a few inches farther back than the bottom, to produce a return with a higher bounce, one that's more like a shot coming from an opponent. The playing surface should be the size of one half of a singles court. High fencing or chicken-wire on all sides and even above the wall itself is desirable; otherwise children and beginners will cover the countryside with tennis balls and spend more time hunting than hitting.

But don't worry. There are few if any perfect walls. The only essential is some kind of horizontal line the height of a tennis net and enough room to swing a racquet. Many a good passing shot was born because the garage wall was too narrow or because somebody had to thread the ball in between the kitchen window and the garbage can and crawl under the car to get every flubbed ball.

It is said that Rod Laver's reflexes are so sharp because, as a boy in Australia, he had to build his own wall out of scraps of wood, and it was so irregular that the ball never came back the same way twice.

The wall is the best way to concentrate totally on one shot at a time. Suppose you've been taught the principles of a topspin backhand, which a pro can show you in ten minutes. After a while you can do it perhaps one time in five, if you're not forced. The only way to build up your percentage enough so you dare to use it in the next club ladder match is to get on the wall and hit 500 of them every day. You can hit 500 shots in 15 minutes or so. Do that every day for a few weeks and you've got it. You can tell when you've got it right because it comes back right. But at first you're going to have to pick up a lot of balls.

Cliff Richey is supposed to have done as many as *five million* shots on the wall to perfect a single stroke. I believe it.

HOW TO LEARN TO LIKE THE WALL

Well, not to hate it anyway.

You'll begin to hate the wall less when you can hit it most of the time. And when you work up your first rat-a-tat rhythm, like punching a bag, you'll begin to enjoy it. Pretty soon you'll be making more shots in half an hour than in two days of gee-whiz family doubles.

Make a game of it. The simplest game is just keeping count. How many shots can you make in a row without hitting below the net line? 10? 100? (Remember that Harold Solomon has points with more than 300 shots.) Do 100 and join the century club. The purist only allows one bounce, but if you're making long drives and don't have a tilted wall, allow two bounces.

Then see how many alternate forehand–backhand shots you can do, and it doesn't count if you hit two forehands or two backhands in a row. Don't cheat—take a full backswing and step into each one, don't slap, and make sure you turn each time and bring the other side toward the wall. Twenty minutes of this drill will leave you soaking wet.

Then when you get to be a real champion, do the ground-shot patterns. First, forehand straight ahead, like a down-the-line shot, back to your forehand; then a cross-court forehand to your backhand; a backhand straight ahead, like a down-the-line backhand, back to your backhand; then a cross-court backhand to your forehand; and so on. Do about 100 complete gambits like that every day for a month and then challenge the Abominable Chopperman at your club to a game. You'll keep him hopping as well as chopping.

Another good wall game is the up-and-back series, if your playing surface is deep enough. Start with two long drives, allowing two bounces; move up to shorter drives, allowing one bounce; move closer still to two half-volleys; and then get in very close for two volleys. You have to be very good to volley against yourself for more than a few shots, but there's no better volleying practice. Ordinary humans can usually manage a forehand-to-forehand or backhand-to-backhand volley, but just try alternating them! See how long you can keep it up without letting the ball touch the ground.

Try target practice, too. Draw a target on the wall just above the net. Better still, draw three of them, one in the center and one on each side. Or draw the face of your Chopperman with his chin on top of the net and try to hit him between the eyes. Hang a tin can on a string to cover his nose, and enjoy the *clang* when you hit it.

Making a bull's-eye on a tennis target takes a lot of practice, because the target has to be inside your head. You can't look at it to sight it as you would a rifle target, because you're looking only at the ball when you hit it, at the *seams* on the ball. Your target in a game, that spot on the court you want to hit, is just the same. The other side of the court must be printed in your head. And yet the accuracy of the great sharpshooters of tennis is, and was, fantastic. Suzanne Lenglen could hit a handkerchief placed anywhere on the other side; and the legendary Czech pro of Bill Tilden's vintage, Karel Kozeluh, could hit a single *coin* almost every time!

On rainy days an empty squash court makes a first-class wall, and if you make sure your shoes are dry and clean, the court will not be harmed. It's easier to keep track of the ball, too. I practiced my first topspin lobs that way. Who knows where the first ones would have gone outdoors?

BALL MACHINES

Electric ball machines are getting more sophisticated all the time, and if your club has one, they're a good variation on the wall. They're especially good for practicing volleys and service returns. For beginners they're much less frustrating than the wall.

One day these electric ball machines will be the ultimate return-of-service trainers. The perfect ball machine of the future will be able to produce all degrees of spin, both of direction and intensity, as well as speed and placement, and will be able to mix up these elements as well as a skillful server. The machine could be computerized so that if your Davis Cup team is playing Sweden, for example, you could program the machine with all of Borg's variations of service and let your team practice hitting a few thousand of them!

The disadvantage of ball machines is that they don't make returns. You get just one shot per ball, and after the machine's ammunition supply is exhausted, you have to reload. Also, you need a whole court for one person, something many clubs can't afford at busy times.

THE FOAM WALL

I predict there will be more foam walls in the future.

Where space is limited, especially indoors, and when many players are practicing, as in a gymnasium, hard walls can send the ball back too fast and too far. A one- or two-inch layer of plastic foam can modulate the return of the ball and can also make volleying practice easier.

Experiment first with the kinds of thicknesses of foam best suited for your own conditions.

One commercial device using foam is called a Ballback, a foam-covered board tilted on an easel-like frame. It returns the ball to about the same spot, even when hit with a variety of speeds. The ones I've seen are so small, however, that only a first-class player could hit them every time.

A GOOD SERVE IS A THOUSAND BUCKETS

You can serve on a wall, but it's never really satisfactory. And you can practice with a friend, taking turns. But the best way to concentrate and to hit thousands of serves is to go out on an empty court with a bucket of tennis balls. (And if they're old balls, make sure they're not soft. If you must use *very* old balls, use old pressureless ones, which stay hard.)

Every serious player should have three basic serves—flat, slice, and twist—one that's fast and straight, one that bounces to the left, and one that bounces to the right. We all know that you hit the flat serve in the middle of the ball, the slice on the right side, and the twist on the left side. And we all know that it's easier said than done.

Most of us learn very early how to do the flat serve and the slice. The slice is a natural stroke; a right-hander hits the ball on the right side, and a left-hander on the left side. The twist, however, is an awkward, basically unnatural stroke because you must swing "around" it in order to hit the upper left side of the ball. Even after a pro shows you how to do it, you will have to make thousands of serves before you can get the ball to go where you want it to go. Thus many people put off learning it until they're old and devious.

To practice serves you need the buckets. You'll never want to use a new serve in a game, even a practice game, until you have a pretty good percentage on it—at least one in two. There's nothing more boring for an opponent than to stand there while you bang double faults into the net.

With the first few dozen buckets concentrate on getting the balls into the little rectangle, with the next few dozen on placing them in the corners, and after that on making the one to the left-hand corner bounce to the left (that is, *your* left, a slice to the deuce court that bounces to the outside) and the one to the right-hand corner bounce to the right (or a twist to the advantage court). This game of tennis solitaire can become quite fascinating.

Try to use a fenced-in court that stands alone, or your balls will drive everyone crazy. You can even use an old broken-surfaced court, since the surface is not important.

BUCKET-COURTS FOR SERVING

Clubs, schools, or tennis camps could put up bucket-courts. They need no special surface, require only one third of the area of a full-sized court, and could be squeezed into corners. (See illustration.)

Each bucket-court needs only one service rectangle, half a net (a piece of an old one), and if it's to be one-sided, fencing in the rear. Of course the ideal bucket-court would have some kind of funnel or drain for pouring balls right into a bucket!

Did I prevent it, or are there hundreds of bucket-courts

DIAGRAM OF A BUCKET-COURT
(superimposed over a court area, dashed lines)

The serving area would take up only about one third the area of a normal tennis court and would require no special surface, except perhaps for the area of the single service rectangle.

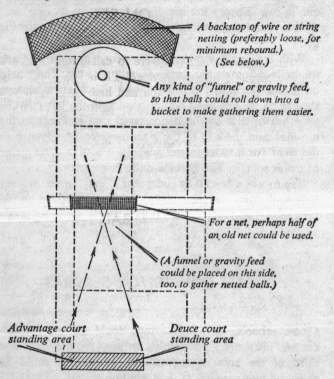

A backstop of wire or string netting (preferably loose, for minimum rebound.)
      (See below.)

Any kind of "funnel" or gravity feed, so that balls could roll down into a bucket to make gathering them easier.

For a net, perhaps half of an old net could be used.

(A funnel or gravity feed could be placed on this side, too, to gather netted balls.)

Advantage court standing area   *Deuce court standing area*

The standing area could be wider if there is room, and possibly should be wider to simulate the wider serving positions of doubles. For the rear netting, perhaps the best material would be the fabric fish-netting that is sometimes used in indoor courts, hung loosely; otherwise hard serves would rebound sharply. A possible variation, if there is room, is a double-ended court, with netting on both ends, and service rectangles on both sides of the net. This also would solve the problem of sun-position.

somewhere? The idea is so simple and logical, but I have yet to see such a court.

A PRIVATE BET ON SERVING

I'll make you a bet. If you were to call me up and ask "What's wrong with my service?" I'll bet I could help you, even if I didn't know you and had never seen you play. I'd say "Just throw the ball up higher and reach for it." In two cases out of three, I'll win the bet.

Every time I tell myself that, it helps. Keep telling it to yourself.

SQUEEZE A BALL

One of the best pieces of training equipment is an old tennis ball. It needs no fuzz and in fact is better with less, but it shouldn't be too soft. Carry one around with you. Keep one by the television set. Squeeze it frequently and squeeze extra hard while watching tennis. Keep one in the car and squeeze it while waiting for your spouse.

Squeezing balls will strengthen your grip enormously and give more power to your whole forearm. Rod Laver is a true believer in ball-squeezing, and look at his left forearm!

DOORWAY TENNIS

I thought up this idea for lecture tours when I couldn't play tennis for weeks on end. It's really tennis isometrics. You can do it anywhere, and all you need is the grip-part of a racquet. Saw off the handle of an old broken racquet just beyond the leather grip. Keep the leather on the grip. Attach a small piece of foam to the end with a rubber band to avoid scratching the door frames. Any other cylinder of comparable size will work as well.

Hold the handle with your usual grip and press it, as if you were making a forehand drive, against the door frame, hard, for just a few seconds, a dozen times. Do the same in the other direction in a backhand position. Repeat the procedure on the top of the door frame in a serve or a smash position. These exercises will strengthen every muscle you use in tennis shots, even in your torso and legs. In fact, you'll strengthen them so much you'll be one-sided unless you always do a slightly lesser amount with your left arm as well. With three minutes of doorway tennis every morning and three more minutes every night, I don't know what a tennis elbow is.

THE BEST TRAINING AID IS A HUMAN BEING

The best training aid of all is a willing partner, and the help will be mutual. It will improve your game to play less and practice more. Instead of playing three sets, try practicing half an hour and then playing two sets.

Everything can be complementary. Service practice for

one gives service-return practice for the other, and vice-versa. Cross-court shots, both backhand and forehand, can go back and forth. Taking turns is the only really satisfactory way to practice lobs and smashes. And the most fun of all is mid-court volleying and half-volleying to each other, trying as in all the other drills to hit it *to* your opponent rather than away. Control is developed either way.

You don't have to practice half an hour every time, but try to do all these shots at least a few times in an extended warm-up before you play. Don't just stand at the baseline and show the people on the terrace how hard you can slam your forehand drive!

10/How To Watch Tennis

*Intelligent watching can improve your
game and increase your enjoyment*

WATCH THE TENNIS, NOT THE BALL

The first thing to remember about watching tennis is that
if you're watching the ball, you're missing the tennis.

Look at any tennis crowd, their heads swinging back
and forth, and you'll see that most spectators just follow
the ball back and forth. They could tell you the score, but
most of them have no idea how the players are playing.

To see the tennis you have to watch the players, and
often *one at a time*. That's the key phrase—one at a time.

The ball is what the players are watching, slightly more
than half the time, with a concentration that has to be almost hypnotic, and of course the action follows the ball,
so you'll watch the ball some of the time. But if you always follow it, you'll watch the player only at the time his
racquet hits it, and then it's too late to see what he did
before he hit the ball and what he does before hitting the
next one. From the moment the ball leaves his racquet, he
is beginning to prepare for the next shot, and what he
does will demonstrate how good a player he is.

First, he'll follow through on his shot, and it's by
watching the follow-through motion that you'll be able to
tell the most about how he's hit the ball and what kind of
spin the ball has as it leaves his racquet. More about that

later. Then he immediately will begin to move toward the next shot, toward the most likely position at the center of the possible returns his opponent can make, already beginning to watch signs in his opponent's position, footwork, shoulders, and backswing that will give him some hint as to where the next shot will go. Sometimes you can tell where the ball will go from his anticipation before you can from your own. Then you'll see how he prepares his stroke, how much backswing he uses, how he steps into the ball, how he makes his stroke, and how all these differ in varying circumstances. Watching this way is very good for your tennis and much more interesting than just looking at the ball.

Probably the most interesting thing is to see how a first-class player improvises strokes under great pressure, often at a dead run, or leaping in mid-air, when all the copybook methods of footwork, backswing, and everything else are wildly impossible. Watch a magician like Nastase perform some of his miracles. You'll never know how in the world anyone could have hit that ball from that position unless you've watched his whole preparation for it from the beginning.

HOW TO SEE THE SPIN

I used to wonder how the commentator knew it was a topspin backhand, or how he knew that the serve was a slice or a twist. You know the theory of it, that the racquet face moves at different angles over the top or to either side of the ball, but at this split second it's going too fast to tell.

The secret is in the follow-through. If the racquet ends up very high on a ground stroke, the shot has topspin; if the racket ends very low, then the shot has slice; and if the racket ends midway, the shot is relatively flat (though many believe, and I agree, that there are few if any completely flat shots).

The follow-through on serves also indicates the type of serve made. If the racquet follows through across the body, far to the left for a right-hander, then it's a slice serve; if it ends up almost straight down, but a trifle to the right, it's a twist. Even a flat serve will come across the body, but not as far across as a slice. The strange follow-through of the twist serve is unmistakable. After observing the follow-through, note how the slice breaks toward the server's left, toward the outside of the deuce court, and how the twist breaks to the server's right, toward the outside of the advantage court. It's interesting to watch whether the server is trying to make the ball break wider, toward the outside, or break inward, perhaps toward the body of the receiver, and how he deliberately varies these. You can be sure the receiver is watching, too!

THE "SERVING-TEST" FOR WATCHERS

If you're more aware of the way each player serves than the way he makes his other strokes, then you're not really watching the tennis, you're watching the ball. Only on the serve is the ball right there with the player and the stroke. On the other strokes it only arrives after the stroke is already made.

HOW TO WATCH FOR FATIGUE AND NERVES

It's interesting to watch the tide of battle change when the better player begins to tire. You can't always tell by the way he acts or the way he walks back into position. He may just be conserving energy.

Watch his playing. Is he reducing his backswing? Is he beginning to slap at the ball? Is he not stepping into it properly? Does he fail to return all the way to a central position after each stroke? These are all clues to fatigue.

But don't confuse these with the energy conservation tactics of wise old foxes like Rosewall and Gonzales, who never take an unnecessary step or make a pointless move. You can learn a great deal from them.

You can detect nervousness, too. One obvious sign is an increase in double faults. But ground strokes also can reflect nervousness, particularly the forehand drive, which often can turn into a tentative swing, a "pulling of the punch," when the player becomes afraid of overhitting.

WHERE AND HOW TO SIT

Do you have a choice? Do I hear laughter? The problem today is to get a seat anywhere. But if you do have a choice, go to the end of the court, not the side, and high enough to be well above the level of the net—in fact, the position at which the main television camera is usually placed, though you don't have to be so far back. This location allows you to follow the strategy of placement, which is mainly lateral, side to side. The height will also let you gauge the depth of the shots.

If you have to be on the side, try to get high enough to see the lateral movement. A seat on the side at ground level is frustrating and almost useless for appreciating lateral strategy. I think of the side benches beside the outer courts at many tournaments, including Wimbledon. However, you do get a close view of stroke production, and you'll be able to hear everything the players say, usually to themselves. Not always for the very young.

How to sit? Quietly, ever so quietly, especially if you're at the end of the court in the sightlines of the players. At many tournaments, including Wimbledon, people are not allowed to walk to their seats during the play, and must wait until the between-game intervals. On several of the outside courts at Paris people walk back and forth directly behind the players. In 1975 this was so bad it seriously affected play, and in 1976 an attempt to stop it by posting officials to these spots met with partial success.

Watch the spectators. You can tell the old hands from the new guys right away. The real tennis people respect the concentration of the players.

And as for cretins who scream in the middle of points, may they and their children always serve double faults, and may all their net cords drop the wrong way.

You'll find all kinds of watchers, all the way down to the idiots who jump up and climb across your seat in search of a beer during match point. You wonder why some of them bother to come at all.

My Know-Nothing Prize of all time, however, goes to an overdressed dowager overheard by my wife at Wimbledon during a doubles match. "Is it like bridge? Is your partner on the opposite side?" Well, it would make for an interesting game!

SHOULD I BRING MY POCKET CALCULATOR?

Well, one of the world's champion tennis-watchers does. Jimmy Jones, the British *Tennis* editor, uses as much science in watching and coaching as he can. That's why English tennis characters call him "the professor."

When Jim is really watching seriously, he brings his calculator and a clip board. The board serves two purposes: (1) to write it all down on, and (2) to hold up and hide the other player, so Jim can concentrate on one player at a time and not be tempted to watch the ball.

What the calculator does is more complicated. Jim punches numbers on every point, giving the degree-of-difficulty of the deciding shot; for example, 20–80 would mean that the player under study is being maneuvered by a difficult ball into a possible forced error. Or if the shot was a sitting duck, then he might punch 90–10. At the end of the match Jones winds up with a column of some 22 numbers for each game. He can then take the whole lot and feed it into a computer.

He did a computer analysis of a match at Philadelphia's Spectrum Stadium between Arthur Ashe and Rod Laver. The computer sheets, compiled by a young London Polytechnic student named Fared Mauthoor, are mind-boggling, but the conclusions don't differ too much from those you might have reached if you had watched the match with a hot dog in one hand and a blonde on the other: (1) Laver won a higher percentage of points with a first service of average speed than with a very fast one; and (2) when he put over a weak first service, he made no points at all, yet with a weak *second* service he won 58 percent of the points.

The computer didn't say why (it wasn't there, was it?),

but Jim suspects it was because Arthur relaxed a bit too much after the first fault. This conclusion proves, at least to me, that Jim's experience and intuition may be a bigger factor than all those electronics.

Jones admits that the science, if it is one, is in the toddler stage. I should think that the way to make it truly scientific would be to take videotape recordings of matches, superimposing a numbered grid (perhaps drawn on a transparent sheet) on the screen as a means of determining exactly where each ball landed. Then you could add to the position the exact angle of the shot (20 degrees left to right); its trajectory, or up-and-down angle (a lob or a flat drive); the direction and degree of spin (calculated on the basis of the opposing player's shot and his follow-through); and its speed (which could be calculated precisely). You could also add facts like whether the shot came from the opponent's backhand, forehand, volley, or whatever, though I think the main point is the motion of the ball itself.

Then you could feed all this complicated information to a computer, together with the reaction of the player under study—whether he hit a winner from the shot, made a forced or unforced error, and so on.

Then your computer should be able to tell you exactly how to hit to any player in its memory file to extract the most errors.

If the material were available to the Davis Cup captain, for example, he might try to pass on the information to his player during the change of courts. "Now remember, Jimmy, just hit a topspin at a 23-degree left-to-right angle at three-quarter speed to segment 13D on the court, and you've got him!"

Would you like to hear *my* reply to that if I were Jimmy? And would the advice be better than some judgment based on playing experience? "You might try changing your pace and your depth to break up his rhythm."

Otherwise we might have to build computers into players, and pre-program them, like cruise missiles.

However, computer analysis may become a valuable training tool for studying players' weaknesses. And if nothing else it may furnish the ultimate loser's excuse. "Okay, Joe, so the score says you beat me 6–, 6–3. But take a look at these computer print-outs. I outplayed you 0.0037876 to 0.0037534. It's right there in black and white!" And who can say you're wrong—except another computer?

HOW TO WATCH AS A PLAYER

If you accept that a spectator should generally take his eyes off the ball, then do you think that a player shouldn't watch the ball either? Is that true?

Surprisingly, it's about half true. *Most players watch the ball too long*.

The tendency of most players is to watch the ball from the time they hit it until their opponent hits it. It's a natural temptation. Don't do it. After you've hit the ball, you know where it's going, and you should begin to look at your opponent, not the ball, *until he hits it*. Thus you should be watching your opponent almost half the time. The rest of the time, after he hits it and until you do, you should be watching the ball very, very closely.

A good player should be able to tell where his opponent is going to hit the ball even *before his racquet touches it*. This is what anticipation is all about, and it can make the difference between getting to the ball and not getting to it.

An interesting audio-visual device is used by Jim Jones and Angela Buxton in their tennis teach-in, which they perform all over Britain. A film was made of Angela with the camera in about the position of her opponent across the net. A ball is hit to her; we see her move toward it, prepare her stroke, and hit. Cut! The film blacks out at the instant the racquet touches the ball.

Each member of the audience has been given a diagram of a tennis court with a grid with lettered segments marked on it, and after viewing the filmed shot, he is asked to write down a letter indicating where the ball would have landed. After 10 or 12 such film clips, the audience is told where the shots actually did land.

An experienced player should be able to tell quite accurately from the position of Angela's feet, her shoulders, and her stroke just about where the ball should go. And if you could watch a few hundred films like this, you'd anticipate much more accurately and begin to watch your opponent more and the ball less.

What is true of one player, however, will not be true of another. Some players disguise their strokes better than others, and some players have an unorthodox style or stroke which makes their shots difficult to anticipate. Pancho Segura's strange but effective two-handed game, both backhand and forehand, was dangerous even to experienced professionals because nobody could tell where the ball would go!

Videotapes or films, either specially made or edited from existing match footage, can be used to study a player's style and strokes by stopping the tape as contact with the ball is made. Action can be replayed in slow motion. The professionals certainly use films to study their opponents, but the tennis club Machiavelli, who is determined to learn to anticipate the shots of all his opponents, can do the same with a tape unit or a Super-8. And watching films could be a devastating tactic for team play skull-practice on any level.

You can practice anticipation yourself while watching tennis at the club or on television. See how often you can guess where the ball will go, just by watching the preparation of the stroke.

There's another kind of anticipation that doesn't involve watching at all—memory anticipation, the knowledge of what your opponent usually does. Memory anticipation works better for club players than for the top pros, who have a much better repertoire of shots.

Some players will always hit backhands cross court, never down the line. If so, you know right where to go, don't you? Some will never serve to the middle line, always to the corner. Many will never hit a topspin lob from the backhand side because they can't, but always will from the forehand when they have a chance. If you can remember all the weaknesses of all your opponents, you can start ambling toward the ball before you even see the shot begin!

BIG-TIME WATCHING

Every tennis player wants to go, at least once, to the big tournaments. True, almost everybody can catch the touring pros not far from home at least once a year. And there's plenty of good watching on television, which offers a much better angle of view than you would have from a poor seat in the auditorium.

But some of us, like me, are addicted and have an irrational urge to be there. I used to live in Forest Hills and didn't miss a National for 14 years, and I haven't missed a Wimbledon for 16.

The best thing about being at a big tournament is seeing what the cameras never do, the early rounds and the new kids. I like to walk around the outer courts watching three or four games here, a set there, and trying to decide which of the nervous boys and girls will make it.

I always prefer the first week of any big tournament to the second. And you can often see the big second week matches on television.

With the tennis boom, the problem now is people. I can remember when the Forest Hill stadium wasn't one-tenth full in the first week. Now even the outside courts are so mobbed it's almost dangerous.

People ask me, "What about Wimbledon? Can you get in?" And I used to say, "Yes, but make it the first week." (That's the last week in June.) All the center-court and number-1-court seats are sold in February, and even then your chances of getting one (in a kind of raffle) are about one in three. Most of the time your check is sent back about May. So, the second week, when all the matches are on these courts, you'd see nothing without tickets. But the first week you used to be able to walk around and see all the players.

Now it is becoming almost impossible from the very first Monday. You stand in line for almost two hours just to get into the grounds, and once you're in, it's almost impossible to see the tennis unless you're seven feet tall because the walk-ways between the outer courts are jammed with people. And if you want to get into the small stands by the outer courts, you may have to wait an hour, or even two hours, in a position from which you can't see anything. And you have to practice what I call hydraulic control. Don't drink anything for hours before you go, because once you do get a seat, if you leave for *any* reason, you can't come back.

In both 1975 and 1976 the general admission gates were closed several times during the first week in mid-afternoon because nearly 40,000 people were jamming the grounds. Even the new 1400-seat stand beside court 14, added in 1976, couldn't begin to absorb the crowd. Hundreds were fainting every day after standing for hours.

People used to come in garden-party clothes. Now the old hands like me bring such survival equipment as raincoat, rain hat or umbrella, sweater, an apple to relieve thirst, and a book to read while sitting for hours in an open stand in cold rain until play resumes. Your only real hope is an hour or two of rain to sluice away the fainthearted. There was not a drop in 1976, the Year of the Sun Bonnet. Some of the dedicated young bring sleeping bags and spend the night outside the admission gates. They're the ones who get the standing-room places.

If your love is this strong or you're slightly unbalanced, and you're ready to endure anything, come ahead. Otherwise, if you want to visit Europe for the tennis in early summer, come the first week of June and go instead to the Paris Open at the Roland Garros Stadium. Most of the same players are there, and you can actually see them play every match, even in the main stadium. All the courts are "clay" (*terre battue*).

And after that, if you really want to see Wimbledon just once to behold the spectacle (and it is one), then go on up to London, go out to the grounds where you'll find scalpers (who have all the tickets) swarming all over, eager to sell you a ticket for about $100 for one seat for one day.

Then go back to your hotel and rent a color television set. The television coverage of Wimbledon is simply incredible by American standards. Every day of the 12 days of the tournament is televised (there is no play on Sunday), from 2 P.M., when play starts, until about 7:30 P.M., and often on two channels at once, so that you can switch from the center court to court 1. And British color television has far more lines in the picture than television in the United States. The difference is about the same as that between magazine and newspaper reproductions, which means you can actually see the ball all the time. I usually watch most of the second week this way.

11 / Court Surfaces and Coverings

A radical change of court surface can break up your tennis club

THE DIFFERENT KINDS OF SURFACES

There are at least 12 different kinds of court surfaces, and most old tennis hands have played on them all. The question, "What kind of surface shall we choose for the new courts?"—or for re-doing the old ones—has caused more fiery debates than any other club issue. One reason for the controversy is that a different surface creates an entirely different game, and a player who is good at one surface may be poor at another. Most of the argument is between loose, movable surfaces (slow) and hard, rigid ones (fast). The pros and cons can be quite complex.

Grass

Lawn tennis was first played in England on croquet lawns. Perfect grass courts on a perfect day are a tennis player's paradise. Gentle to feet and spirit, grass is far less tiring to play on; shoes and balls last far longer on it (though they do get green); and you can fall on it, roll on it, lie on it, even eat on it.

Because grass produces the lowest bounce in tennis, and a sliding one, too, it's preferred by the serve-and-volleyers, the "big game" players. It's a fast surface, and deadly to the Forever players-by-attrition, like Solomon and Dibbs.

Today real grass is totally impracticable for any club that doesn't have (as my English club does) a trained staff of experts to care for it and baby it. Perfect grass is marvelous; anything less than perfect is unplayable, weedy, scruffy, and too soft, and produces irregular bounces, which is why Forest Hills finally changed to "clay" in 1975. Even with the best care, grass courts are playable only about one third of the time. At our English club they were open from about the first of May to the end of September, but even during that time they were closed to play about half the time, either for maintenance or because they were wet and therefore too soft.

All Wimbledon is still grass. The center court is used for only two weeks of the year, and at the end of the two weeks it is almost unplayable and needs months to recuperate. The finals are always played on tattered grass, the baselines almost as bare as clay.

All continental European players hate grass. I've never seen a grass court anywhere on the continent. "Grass," they say, "is for cows."

Some of the new artificial grass surfaces, like astro-turf, or the various forms of synthetic carpeting usually used indoors are very pleasant for playing and often very expensive.

Clay

Clay used to mean real clay or hard-packed earth which sometimes contained at least some clay. Now it refers to almost any loose or movable surface, as opposed to a completely hard, rigid surface like concrete.

Most modern clay courts are designed for two basic purposes: water drainage and a yielding surface on which players can slide. Few of them contain any real clay at all.

Real clay becomes muddy and slippery when wet, and dusty when too dry. Good clay construction is often more than a foot deep, with layers of rubble and pebbles at the bottom, followed by cinders or other porous material to allow drainage, and a final layer of granular but nonsoluble material made variously of ground shale or brick and labeled with such commercial names as En Tout Cas or Har Tru (the name of the new Forest Hills surface made of powdered granite). Most of the courts require regular maintenance—occasional rolling, and usually daily brushing or dragging and sprinkling. Good ones are playable very quickly after a rain.

All continental European tournaments are played on these clay surfaces, which the French call *terre battue* (beaten earth). Players who use sliding as a playing tactic are frightened by rigid surfaces like blacktop or concrete, which they consider dangerous. If you're used to sliding and try a hard, fast one on concrete, you can have a bad fall and even break a leg. I prefer a yielding surface for this reason.

Though you can slide your feet on clay, the ball doesn't slide very much and instead bounces up high. Thus, clay is a slow surface. Conversely, you cannot slide your feet on a wooden floor, but the ball slides on it, and wood is considered a fast surface.

The official genius of tennis, James Van Alen, who invented the tie-breaker and other scoring systems, said after the first clay, or Har Tru, Forest Hills, "They've got to put more skid into it. This surface makes it too hazardous for a man to come to the net." Van Alen didn't mean "hazardous" in the sense that the man would fall down (he'd be more likely to do that on grass, especially if it were a bit damp), but rather that the sitting-duck quality of the bounce made it easier for his opponent to pass him at the net. Van Alen wanted more skid for the ball, or a faster surface. And of course Orantes, a clay-court player, won that first clay Forest Hills in 1975.

You could tell, in 1976, that the groundskeepers had been using rollers on those new courts. They were surely faster, and the results were dramatic. Harold Solomon, considered by many tennis buffs to be the best clay-court player in the country, was put out in the first round by young Billy Martin, and the last slow-court specialists, Orantes, Kodes, and Dibbs, were all knocked out in the quarter finals by, respectively, Borg, Connors, and Vilas, all fast-court players.

Hard Courts

Hard courts include the concrete of California and the asphalt-based blacktops. The main disadvantage of the early hard courts (in addition to the problem of rigidity) was lack of drainage and therefore puddles after a rain. To solve this problem of drainage the new hard courts have a porous surface and drainable underlayers. There are now many plastic and porous concretes and blacktops with names like Tennisquick, Grassphalte, Greenset, and so on. Their great advantages are that they require almost no maintenance, they always give a true bounce, and they are playable all winter, whereas even the modern clay courts (or all that I know about) usually are out of action after the frost gets into them.

Our Swiss club almost split in two over the issue of kind of surface to use for re-doing our courts. Should we use a new green plastic surface or put in new clay or *terre battue* courts to replace the old clay? We compromised by doing some in *terre battue* and some in a plastic called Greenset. In summer the clay surface is much more popular, and many players refuse to go on the plastic at all. All players who broke their legs skiing the previous winter, usually quite a few, are advised to stay off the plastic the first season. But the plastic courts now allow us, for the first time, to play outdoors all winter.

Remember that courts planned primarily for winter play should be oriented at right angles to those planned for summer play. Otherwise the low winter sun will be in your eyes.

An interesting variation of the concrete court is used in many parts of Europe, including the new courts at Lew Hoad's pleasant tennis club near Malaga in southern Spain. Smooth round pebbles are embedded in the top of the concrete. It's smoother on the feet and less damaging if you fall. (Pure speculation! I didn't fall, not once!)

Wood

Wood, the traditional indoor surface, is still used in gymnasiums and armories in many places. One big indoor tournament in England is played on the five wooden courts at Queens Club. Wood is the fastest surface of all. The ball hits, slides, and "comes through" very rapidly. However, the bounce is always true and less likely to react to spin. After years of playing on it at Queens, I still dislike wood, but it's the favorite of some players.

Fabric

The touring pros are doing one-night-stands everywhere now, from ice rinks to ballrooms, and they bring their courts with them. Made of heavy canvas-like fabric with the lines marked on them, these courts are unrolled like carpets and stretched tightly. The surface eliminates some of the sliding of the wood. Have court, will travel!

COVERINGS

Indoor courts are popping up everywhere now, like mushrooms. Some, the nylon pressure-balloons, even *look* like mushrooms. We put up three of these in Lausanne, two courts in each, and they're reserved all winter from dawn till late at night. I've played in them for several years. Erected in winter over clay courts, they're taken down every spring and presto! Outdoor courts! There are no struts or rafters to hit. The light is gentle and translucent in daytime and fluorescent by night. But beware of warm, sunny days. If it's 70° outside, it's 96° inside. Our courts are heated, but not air-cooled.

The French now have a "fabric-on-wood"—a kind of tent stretched over a wooden frame. There are all kinds of shell-concrete umbrellas, and every sort of building, from big quonset huts to elaborate pleasure-domes with carpeted courts, a sauna, swimming pool, bar, and restaurant. I've played in places in New England that are like complete indoor country clubs.

PLATFORMS ARE FOR WINTER

Is there still a live tennis player who hasn't heard about platform tennis? When we first played platform in the 1940's on Long Island, I had to explain to people what it *was* and that it wasn't that paddle tennis game that children played on the beach.

Once played only in the New York commuting area, it's growing so fast now all over the country and even abroad that it may overtake tennis.

Tennis clubs in cold climates used to close down in the winter. No more. Even snow doesn't stop platform tennis. Far cheaper than indoor courts and much better for your tennis game than squash, the platforms are in use all winter long. Platform isn't "wristy" like squash and uses almost all the same strokes as tennis. At our Long Island club, where we had both squash and platform, the platform was much more popular.

Some even prefer it to tennis because it's such an equalizer. Almost all the members of a club can play it together. The caste-system hardly applies. Man and wife sometimes play on the same court together for the first time.

It all started with that beach paddle tennis game. Any racquet player could see the flaw in that game. Because the net is half as long as a tennis net and the distance to the net only half as far as on a tennis court, all you had to do was get to the net. Nobody could pass you or lob over you. One volley or smash and the point was over.

Platform tennis was invented almost by accident. James Cogswell and Fessenden Blanchard built a paddle court in the Cogswell back yard in the New York suburb of Scarsdale and put a chicken-wire netting around it to cut down on ball-chasing. They discovered the game was much improved by allowing balls to be taken off the wire. Instantly the net man's advantage disappeared. Volleys and smashes could be picked off the wire on the rebound, almost as in squash.

Today the proper courts have the netting tightly stretched, and there are snow gates at the bottom to open for snow-pushing. Since the court is only about one third the area of a tennis court, four healthy platformers can push off a sizeable snowfall and still have time for a few sets before lunch. I've done it many times.

The only difference in the rules, aside from the rebound, is that you're only allowed one serve, and if the serve is too hard, you can take it off the wire.

Tennis players can transfer their skills to platform tennis immediately. For instance, when we started platform at our Long Island club in the 1940's, Don McNeill and Frank Guernsey had recently won the Forest Hills doubles championships. (Platform is almost always played as doubles.) Don and Frank, both very pleasant characters, were visiting our club and were invited to try platform for the first time. Our two best players beat them 6–2 the first set. The second set Don and Frank won 6–2. Later, in 1953 and 1954 they became national platform champions.

Feron, the New York racquet maker, produced a platform racquet which had strings like a tennis racquet but a short handle. I had one of the first ones, and it became known as the Whispering Snickersnee because it was relatively silent. The Feron racquet was finally (and I think wisely) ruled out, and the game is now played entirely with paddles, which last for years and require no stringing and almost no attention. A single sponge rubber ball is used, and the real sophisticates now have electric ball warmers.

Platform is played in clothes that look more like ski clothes, and many clubs have built glassed-in "chalets" in the midst of their courts so members can watch comfortably. Sometimes there's an open fire or a stove, and hot coffee and soup. It's a hearty and rosy-cheeked atmosphere.

Clubs that want offical rules and information about building courts can apply to the American Platform Tennis Association, 52 Upper Montclair Plaza, Upper Montclair, N.J. 07043.

12 / How to Stretch Tennis Courts

Maybe your tennis club is bigger than you think

STOP THAT ANGRY MUTTERING

Once you have honed your game into a deadly weapon and are ready to defeat or mesmerize everyone, you may discover you have the problem of most players ever since the beginning of the great tennis boom: you don't have any place to play.

Most tennis clubs today are clusters of courts surrounded by angry muttering. True, from a block away the first thing you hear are squeals of strained laughter and the plip-plop of tennis balls. Only as a member will you hear the undertone.

> *"There must be a better way to run a tennis club!"*
> *"Two hours waiting around and I haven't fired a shot!"*
> *"Why do they get to play all the time?"*

What can you do? Sell off the club to make half of one hole for a golf course or to build a drive-in hamburger stand? Take up croquet?

Not yet, there's hope. True, I've never seen a tennis club turned into a bower of cuddly bliss. It isn't ring-around-a-rosy they're playing. All tennis players are dedicated to the attack and destruction of each other in every way possible with racquet, balls, and brain-boggling.

However, it is possible to stop most of the angry muttering, and there are ways to stretch tennis courts to fit too many members. You can bring a cease-fire to the Clubhouse War.

THE MUTTERINGS ARE MORE IN MAY

If your club has enough courts for everybody in May, it doesn't have enough members. If it doesn't have enough courts in August, it doesn't have enough courts.

In the spring you and every other wistful hacker and chopper get new resolve. Let the warm sun begin to shine, and you begin to think, "This is my year. This is the big break-through. Get out there now! Hit the ball! Work!"

So you rush to the club only to find that all the courts are signed up till dark, except that one down in the hollow that's still under water. You join one of the groups of angry mutterers and wonder if you should find a different club. And if you look around, you discover that all the other clubs are crawling with angry mutterers who can't play either.

In a month or two the frenzy dies down. People go on vacation, and it's warm enough to swim. And some of the springtime ambitions are put off till next year.

But if by June there still aren't enough courts, you've got a problem, and the only thing is to stretch the ones you've got.

SIX COURT STRETCHERS

Don't confuse court-stretching with line-stretching, which is the way some people make out-balls into in-balls.

1. Do you need to change your watchdog

At your club, who decides when the members can play? After a rain, for example, on many kinds of court, somebody will have to decide when people can play. (If you have nobody to decide this, people may just run out and play anyway and ruin the courts. Then you won't have any to stretch.)

The rule should be: *The watchdog must be a tennis player and not a maintenance man.* He must be someone who likes to play tennis and who likes tennis players. The maintenance man or courtkeeper regards all tennis players as his natural enemies. They are the people who mess up the nice courts that he keeps. At his dream club no one ever plays tennis, and the courts just sit there, lovely, virginal, untouched by human foot. He will do everything he can to keep you from playing as long as possible. And this is in conflict with the purpose of a tennis club, which is to have the largest number of players playing the most possible tennis and having the most possible fun.

The guidelines must be: Okay, play, if the courts just get messed up a bit, but don't play if they may be permanently damaged. And if your courtkeeper has become a fussy old dictator, fire him and get a new one.

Only at a grass-court club must the courtkeeper have some authority, because he has to be a true expert. Grass courts, which are so beautiful and so pleasant to play on, are so fragile that one set played at the wrong time can ruin them for a season. But this is a problem mainly in England, the last stronghold of real lawn tennis.

2. Have a good sign-up system for reserving courts

The only sign-up system that works is one that is time-based rather than play-based; i.e., a player signs up for a definite time and plays a fixed length of time, like an hour, rather than for one set or two sets. A set can last from 20 minutes to two hours. One of my clubs had a play-based system that was so often abused that the cliché joke was "What's your score"—"One-all." Unscrupulous characters could play all afternoon, using a kind of double-entry score, one for themselves and one for the rest of us.

The best system requires all club members to have name tags or plates that can be placed on a board divided into 15-minute segments for each court. (One of my clubs used little magnetic plates with the names in dymo tape of varying colors. Juniors, for instance, were in a different color.) On very busy days, these plates are removed for the day after one playing session. In other words, if you've played once during the day, you don't play again until everybody else has played once. The name-plate system is also handy to make sure everybody had paid dues, since you don't get your plate in the spring until you've paid. Someone has to be in charge of this system—someone who is both fair and tough.

3. Have a datemaker

Sometimes the bunch-ups can be avoided by spreading the players over a wider time span, and one good way to do this is to have someone arrange playing dates. Some clubs have a paid secretary who combines the job of club manager with the functions of a match secretary. And some very rich or very big clubs hire someone who does only matchmaking. The bigger the club, the more you need someone like this. He or she can act as a central clearing house, keeping track of which courts are available and who wants to play, often making up matches between people who don't yet know each other, filling in fourths for doubles, and so on. The person must be sufficiently tennis-wise to know who can and who will play with whom, and can tell you things like: "Well, no, all the courts are reserved at two, but if you can make it at one-thirty there are three about your speed who are looking for a fourth—" So you play.

If you club can't afford a full-time match secretary, try using volunteers. An energetic tennis committee could arrange for people to take turns holding down a central telephone or clearing desk, at least during the most crowded times.

4. Have plenty of training walls

Encourage people to warm up on the wall so that all their time on the court will be playing time. And on days of complete log-jam, players can at least get a work-out. Half an hour on the wall might leave them limp, but it will improve their game more than two hours of playing.

5. Regulate the young, but don't abolish them

The first thought of most tennis committees is to throw out all juniors when the courts get crowded. However, remember that the best players on your club team five years from now will be those little kids when they're about two feet taller. They will be, that is, if you help them. You may have to limit their play on Saturdays and Sundays and summer evenings after six. But try to have some kind of merit system to give extra playing time to the really ambitious juniors who are serious about tennis and willing to work hard at it. One of my clubs gave these juniors tags of a special color for court reservations, allowed them to play during restricted times, and encouraged them to play with adults. There were also special coaching and training sessions on certain weekdays after school.

6. Encourage doubles

Many people, like me, would rather play doubles than singles, but almost everyone prefers doubles to not playing at all. The simplest way to have more doubles is to make it easier to reserve courts for four, and to give the foursomes longer time to play. For example, allow members to reserve doubles courts several days in advance, but singles courts only on the playing day. And if you allow an hour for singles reservations, then allow an hour and a half for doubles.

One practical difficulty in a large club is just to get people organized into fours. Here are some ways to do it.

13 / Tennis Fun and Games

*Some ways to mix members, get everyone
to play, and have more fun at your club*

Some days you come home from the club feeling unfulfilled. Somehow you've missed connections or just played
with the same old people, and you wish you could have a
little more variety and relax and laugh a bit more. The
object, after all, is exercise, sociability, and joy.

Here are some proved ways to shake things up.

CLUB DAY OR DICTATOR DOUBLES

Many English tennis clubs have what is usually called
Club Day, and it is probably the most effective way to get
members of a large club to mix and to have a fine social
afternoon doing it. (Our club in Surrey, which is in the
suburbs of London, had Club Day every Saturday afternoon, even in winter. Some of my best friendships in England grew out of these afternoons of tennis.)

Each week a different member volunteers to be the
nonplaying organizer. Everyone turns up at a fixed time
every week, and as people arrive, the organizer or "dictator" divides them into fours and sends them onto the
courts that have been reserved for the operation. (The
event doesn't have to take up *all* the courts, although all
were used at our club.) The organizer uses his own judg-

ment in making up the fours into mixed doubles, men's doubles, and women's doubles.

Each group of four plays one short set, maximum 6–5, and then returns to the central point (perhaps the club terrace), where the organizer reshuffles them, trying as far as possible to have each person play each time with three different people. (You can write down scores if you want, but we never did.) After about two hours of combined play (perhaps four short sets) and chit-chat on the terrace between sets (which is really part of the object), there's a break for refreshments. (In England for tea, of course.) After the break, people make up their own games, and the nonplaying dictator can play now too.

The key to the success of a Club Day is the organizer or dictator. Without him, and it is quite often a her, people just stand around, especially if it's a big club with a sizable annual turnover and the members don't yet know each other. The main problem in getting Club Days started is signing up organizers, and at first the tennis committee should appoint its own members in rotation to do it. Once the idea catches on, every Club Day regular will feel an obligation to be the organizer once a season.

One big advantage is that because you play only one short set with each group, you're never stuck with a bad game for long. If you're not well-matched, it's all over in 15 minutes or so, you've had a few laughs, and you go back for another try.

Even if you're a brand new member, a few weeks of going to Club Days will get you started. You'll see who's in your class, and the others will see how *you* play.

THE INSTANT ROUND-ROBIN TOURNAMENT

This kind of tournament requires no previous arrangements, draws, or massive telephoning. Everybody arrives at a fixed time with or without a partner. Names of those without partners are put in a hat, and partners are drawn. Pairs are divided into groups of six or seven, and each pair plays each of the other five or six pairs in their group in a short match of seven games, returning after each match to the central desk to report the number of games won. The pair with the greatest number of games is the winner of the group. Group winners then have a one-set elimination tournament; for example, if there are four groups, then the group winners play a pair of semi-finals and those winners play a final. The whole operation can be played in a morning or an afternoon.

This tournament is the one best suited to the sliding handicap described in chapter 3. The sliding handicap provides instant leveling and considerable merriment, and you really have to be good to get a 7–0 score if you're playing the last five games with 30–love against you.

The tournament is called an "American tournament" in England, though I never heard of it at any of my American clubs.

CHANGE-YOUR-PARTNERS OR SQUARE-DANCE TENNIS

This tournament is another British variation of the "American" round-robin tournament, and if played as mixed doubles, it is perhaps the best sex-mixer I know.

No advance arrangements are necessary, just have everybody come, and then draw partners out of a hat. No need to worry if you've got the Biggest Liability partner, everything will soon change. Partners split every seven-game match—losers stay on the court and go to opposite sides, and winners move to the next court and split. Each player keeps an individual score of number of games won.

Here's how it works with 16 players and four courts. Man-A and woman-B are playing man-C and woman-D on court 2, and they win 4–3. Losers C and D stay on court 2, but split, one going on each side. Winner man-A goes up to court 3 to join the loser woman of court 3, and winner woman-B goes down to court 1 to join the loser man of court 1, and so on. Soon everyone will have played as a partner with just about every player of the opposite sex in the club.

You can play this tournament with sliding handicaps if you like, but the splitting of winners and losers usually equalizes the competition.

If you have more men than women, then any two men playing together against a mixed pair start with 15 against them. If you have more women than men, then any two women playing against a mixed pair receive 15 each game.

No semi-finals or finals are necessary. The man and the woman with the highest individual scores are the winners.

LONG-TERM ROUND ROBINS

The long-term round-robin tournament lasts a whole season. Teams arrange their own times to play, and do so at their own convenience.

At the beginning of the season, people sign up for the tournament in teams of four—four men, or four women, or two men and two women for mixed. Why teams of four rather than two? When teams have alternate players, they can play matches in spite of vacations, business trips, and so on. Teams are divided into groups of six or seven, and definite playing deadlines are given; for example, the number 2 team must play the number 3 team in its group by May 20th or default. Both teams agree on a date, and they play two short sets, or a maximum score of 6–5, 6–5. Each team is given points for each game won. If both players in either pair are of the bottom class, they receive 15 in each game. At the end of the season there is a playoff of group leaders.

TOURNAMENTS FOR SPECIAL GROUPS

Clubs everywhere have doubles tournaments for special groups—father-and-son, mother-and-daughter, brother-and-sister, and men's veteran. (Veteran events are popular only with men, because no woman wants to admit she's over 45.)

An interesting variation is the "Over-70" doubles, which has always been the final tournament at our Swiss club and is always the most popular of the year. The only requirement is that the combined ages of the two male contestants be 70 or over, all juniors counting as 20. So, if you're playing with a junior, you have to be at least 50. The final is often a spirited battle of the hottest early-20's player and his father or some other old crocodile against two late-30's players.

A GOOD THREE-HANDED GAME

Two-against-one tennis is never as good as singles or doubles, but it sometimes seems necessary, especially on those days when the clubhouse is closed, and it's too cold to sit around and wait.

In all three-handed games, of course, the singles player hits to the doubles court, and the doubles players hit to the singles court. Because the doubles players usually can control the net, and therefore have the advantage, it is best to play in rotation. The singles player always serves, and to keep the score from becoming too complicated, the only games that count are service wins. Each player is on absolutely even terms with the others.

Here's how the game works. The singles player serves and wins. Score, 1–0–0. The server rotates clockwise to receive in the deuce court, the player who was in the deuce court moves over to the advantage court, and the advantage receiver moves across to serve. (The server is always on the same side, so if there's a nasty sun, keep him on the good side.) The server loses, and the score remains 1–0–0. The players rotate again. The player who was in the advantage court now serves, and he wins. Score, 1–0–1. And so on.

For some reason, three-handed games are called "Canadian doubles" in England, which probably means that the Canadians have never heard of them!

A TEN-GAME SINGLES ROUND ROBIN

This is the only one of the fun games I haven't played, but it seems simple and self-explanatory.

The players are divided into the usual round-robin groups of 5 or 6, each one to play each member of his group. The first player to reach ten games wins the individual match, but because the only scoring is by number of games won, theoretically you could lose all your matches 9–10 and still win the tournament.

If there are several groups, there is the usual play-off, usually a normal three-set match.

All the above games are for reasonably responsible occasions. But even tennis players have their wild moments, and there can be some very wild tennis.

14 / Cocktail Tennis

Can joy be unrestrained at a tennis club?
Here are some uninhibited games for your
once-a-year day

Anyone who plays tennis at any club knows that tennis is a matter of life and death, of tears, rage, desperation, humiliation, and even terror and hatred for at least part of the club population. In fact, it is a haven for all the more violent and unpleasant human emotions.

I know some players who haven't laughed or even smiled on a court for years. Sometimes after a match I've wondered if I should remove their belts or the laces from their sneakers, and keep sharp objects away from them, I knew one lovely and athletic blonde who would cry real tears if I beat her. And by beating her, I mean only having a higher score. For some of these sad players there may be nothing we can do, but there are borderline cases we may be able to save.

Even the most dedicated and determined tennis clubs do have their wild moments, if only to gather strength for the next relentless offensive. This is the time for us to act, all of us who think tennis is fun.

Let's assume that the time has arrived, that once-a-year day, the season opener, the club cocktail party. That skinny fellow who jogs ten miles a day and drinks nothing but buttermilk may relent and have a sip of lager. So will the thin-lipped old hacker who eats nothing but yoghurt, whole-grain cereal, and organically grown vegetables and always wins the C tournament with a nasty backhand chop.

If you want to use the courts at all in a situation like this, you will have to act. You will have to contrive something so nutty that even the tennis monomaniacs can't take it seriously. Like, for instance—

THE TRUMPET TOURNAMENT OR PISTOL TENNIS

The only extra equipment needed for this tournament is a trumpet, a whistle, a siren, a starting pistol, or anything else you can hear above the squeals and grunts of tennis players. And a watch.

Members, not necessarily sober, are rounded up, paired off, and written down in a very rough round robin. Mixed pairs are best, but don't quibble. Any two warm bodies will do.

All play begins at the same moment, when the trumpet blows or the pistol fires, and must continue in a spirited manner for at least 8 minutes and not more than 18—a time that must be decided purely at random after the start of play by a timekeeper who cannot be aware of what is going on. In fact, if he is in the bar and three sheets to the wind, so much the better.

When this time arrives, perhaps 11 minutes and 9 seconds after the start of play, the trumpet blows or the pistol fires, play stops, *and all odd-numbered scores are DOUBLED.*

If you've ever played the trumpet tournament, you know the stormy emotions that arise when you stand at 5–6, know the trumpet may blow at any second, and are serving to win at 40–30. Do you really *try* to win, and thus have the score of 6–6 instead of 10–6? Is it a sin not to try? There have been cases of balls being hit, accidentally, over the clubhouse (Note: use old balls), of players who suddenly develop incurable cramps, and of topspin drives hit sideways. But one mustn't deliberately try to lose points, and those who do are punished; for example, you might be deprived of an olive in your second martini.

Several rounds can be played, as many as seem to be advisable or safe at the time.

The winners always receive loving cups. Full.

TWO-COURT COCKTAIL TRIPLES

This game of triples is a legendary game, often talked about, but rarely played or seen. Because it is primarily a spectator sport, it should be played at a club that has at least two adjoining and somewhat parallel courts which have no fence (or at least not a high fence) between them and are visible (if only through a bibulous haze) from the clubhouse terrace or porch.

Some say it was invented at the old Seminole Club, in Forest Hills, in its golden days, in the 1940's, where all the above conditions prevailed, including the bibulous haze, of which I was once a hazy part.

However, any two tennis courts that are within striking or running distance of each other can be used, and the rules can be slightly bent to fit.

Obstacles between the courts, such as an umpire stand or a parked car of unknown ownership, must be retained to create a kind of obstacle course. An umpire is necessary, and he must possess courage and qualities of leadership. Ideally he should sit in an umpire stand *between* the two courts, and if so, should wear protective clothing, such as a motorcycle helmet or a fencing mask, and a referee's whistle. Because it is difficult to use a whistle and a fencing mask simultaneously, the ideal equipment would be a mask with a whistle-gate, which might look like a beekeeper's hat.

Balls actually striking the umpire must be played let, even when they bounce in. This rule was necessary because participants tended to play balls *off* the umpire.

Choose six relatively clear-headed volunteers (no one should be forced to play) including sturdy women, if any are available. They need not be dressed entirely in tennis clothes, but they must be either barefooted or wearing tennis shoes or rubber boots to protect the courts.

Scoring is similar to ordinary tennis. In fact the only thing the players need to remember is that *every third ball must be hit into the adjoining court.* This is, of course, easier said than done. Thus, the server in court 1 serves into the normal deuce rectangle of court 1, the receiver hits back a normal doubles shot into any part of the doubles area of court 1, and any one of the three-or-less occupants who are still there hits this *third* ball into the opposite, or receiver's, side of court 2, the *other* court, where, by this time, at least one of the three enemy players hopefully is. He hits the fourth ball into the serving side of court 2. An opponent there hits the fifth ball to the receiving side of court 2. The next shot is the sixth ball, and therefore is hit to the serving side of court 1, the original court. And so on.

The server continues to serve out the game in court 1 in the normal way, first to the deuce rectangle, then to the advantage rectangle, but the serve may be received by any of the three opponents who happens to be around. Serves pass in rotation to each of the six players and to each of the four serving positions on both sides of the two courts. Serves are always made within one court area; i.e., the server in court 1 never serves into the rectangle in court 2.

If a player fails to hit the ball into the other court on the third shot of each three-shot "salvo" (as it is called), the umpire blows his whistle, and that side loses the point.

As in normal doubles, there are no rules about where the players must stand, except that they must always be on their own sides of the net (or nets, in this case). It is entirely a matter of strategy and tactics. Some teams (or troikas) operate on an anarchistic or every-man-for-himself principle, but the most successful are disciplined, with a captain or third-back calling signals and marshalling his forces. Some choose to keep one player in each court and have one team member (often the captain himself) run from one court to the other. This two-court player is sometimes called the short-stop or alley-runner, or in England the tram-liner.

Duration of the match depends partly on the condition of the players (sometimes deplorable), but the classical set (or triple wicket) is six games, which allows each player to serve once. If the games are then 3–3, a tie-breaker can follow, allowing two serves for each of the six servers.

Some clubs allow substitutions, and keep a bench or dugout beside the courts (but never between them). Some even use a penalty box for flagrant offenses or personal attacks. Such penalties can reduce the team to two, one, or even *no* players.

All players, especially those competing for the first time, should be spoken to calmly in advance. The game can easily degenerate into a kind of scuffle *if not played with dignity*.

The game is growing, but there is some debate as to whether this is a good sign or a bad one.

HAREM TRIPLES

For those who don't have an adjoining-court situation, another good festival or semi-orgy game is Harem Triples. This three-to-a-side game requires only one doubles court, no special equipment, and very little instruction—only perhaps a little intimidation.

Some say harem triples serves a high moral purpose because it proves a man is better off with one wife than two. Others find it shows just the opposite—that a man is far happier with two wives than one. Others claim it proves both and separates the men from the boys.

Each team consists of one man and two women. The man always covers the singles court, never the alleys, and the two women cover the whole doubles court. Return shots must always alternate (as in table-tennis doubles) so that on each side the man hits every other shot. The man always serves to the other man, and the women to the other women. This avoids the common complaint of women against mixed doubles, that they are forced to stand there and have men swatting those macho serves at them.

Each of the six players serves a full game, in sequence. The first woman serves to the woman in the deuce court, who returns the ball anywhere in the opposite singles court, where it is hit by the man, who returns to the singles court to the other man, who returns to the doubles court to either woman, who returns to the doubles court to the opposing women, who return to the man, and so on.

Scoring can be the same as any doubles, with normal sets. Or if people are impatient, scoring can be done as in the previous triples—one serve to each, plus a tie-breaker at 3–3 if needed.

LIBERATION OR BOSS-LADY TRIPLES

This game is a natural transposition of harem triples, with one woman and two men to a side. It appeals to a certain type of power-hungry woman and, as any man can tell you, arouses emotions better left unaroused.

Ball boys and ball girls are permitted for any of these events, though there are some who feel that children should be kept as far as possible from this sort of thing.

MISCELLANEOUS DEPRAVED GAMES

If yours is a club that stops at nothing, there is almost no limit to the kinds of unorthodox tennis that can be played by members whose inhibitions have been temporarily dissolved.

These include *piggy-back-mixed,* with the man doing the running and the woman the hitting (and the spurring on); *wrong-handed doubles,* with right-handers playing left-handed, and vice-versa; and still more depraved, wrong-handed doubles played on a singles court (which creates greater intimacy); *roller-skate tennis* (rubber-tired skates and hard courts only); and numerous forms of *prop-handicap tennis*, such as "Hey, garçon!" in which players must carry a tray full of crockery on one hand (the server is allowed two hands, but must pick up his tray immediately after serving) or *hustler tennis,* in which players are wearing various forms of Bobby-Riggs-type costumes—like a raincoat and galoshes and carrying a suitcase, or, in the case of women, wearing floor-length dresses, with bustles, and carrying parasols.

On the other hand, many feel that it is better simply to get on with the serious drinking.

15 / How to Use Tennis to Further Your Ends

A dastard's guide to tennismanship, how to use it, and how to keep others from using it on you

TENNIS CAN GET YOU MORE THAN YOU DESERVE

All tennis lovers know that the game is an admirable end in itself. At its best it can be an unconfined joy, an ecstasy second only to one.

However, the unscrupulous can use tennis to further their ends. Shrewd and ruthless tennismanship, quite separate from the simple gamesmanship used for winning games, can result all too often in rapid rises up the social ladder, advantageous marriages (abundant either financially, social-registerally, or erotically), lascivious affairs, and, perhaps most often of all, meteoric rises up through the business world and rich financial success.

Or, briefly, tennismanship can give one much more than one deserves.

Is tennismanship a perversion of tennis? Yes, it is. But as a tennis player you must know about it, if only to prevent others from doing it to you.

And for those who prefer terms like chairperson, or herstory for history, the sister-term tennispersonship or tenniswomanship is there for the taking. Whatever you want to call it, girls, it will certainly work for you, too.

TENNIS CAN MAKE YOU POSH

Or if you're already posh, tennis can make you posher. Tennis can help anyone to rise socially and to rise fast.

Though tennis is now developing a split social personality, it is still possible to use the old and perhaps dying one for instant social acceleration. And if you intend to do it, you'd better do it quickly, before Team Tennis, Las Vegas promoter-type gladiatorial matches, hustling, and tough-baby tennis thuggery turn our gentleman's, and gentlewoman's, pastime into a racquet-wielding prizefight biz.

But not quite yet. The Establishment still clings to the old image, and there are still nostalgic memories of social graces, whitewashed-brick country clubs, and grassy lawns at Newport, Southhampton, and (once, alas!) Forest Hills. One still speaks of the Gentlemen's Singles Championships of the All-England Lawn Tennis and Croquet Club. (That's men's Wimbledon, Mac.) Tennis players, usually the old-fashioned rather languid types, still appear in the chic perfume ads and decorate the publicity photos of luxury sport cars. (They're all models, of course, who have to be taught how to hold a racquet.)

Some of the illusion is still there—that tennis players are ladies and gentlemen. "People who are good at games are rally *our* kind of people, my deah," and lawn tennis is till one of the best games to be good at. And, as the English say, it is always better to create the impression that tennis is merely *one* of the games that one is good at. One really mustn't be too keen, must one? Or, in vintage Ivy League, don't run it out, lad.

There's no quicker way for a kid from the wrong side of the tracks to get on the other side than to be a good tennis player. A fast course in clothes and which-forkmanship, along with all that hitting against the wall, will multiply many times a person's chances of marrying far up the ladder or joining the upper escadrille of that very special corporation.

He doesn't even have to be good enough to play at Forest Hills. In fact if he's good enough to play there, but not good enough to win the big prizes, he may just become a tennis bum following the tennis circuit and picking up the crumbs, and the only people he'll meet then will be other tennis bums.

HOW TO SUCCEED IN BUSINESS THE TENNISMANSHIP WAY

There are more and more companies now in which it is harder and harder to rise unless you *are* a tennis player. If you don't play at all, you'll simply be left out of the tennis lunches and country-club afternoons. You'll be the outsider, the guy who doesn't play—the way it used to be with golf.

Prospective assistants are sometimes informally "interviewed" on a tennis court. "Well, I mean, Charlie, he's gotta know the business, too, but if there are two guys who both know the business, why not pick the guy who can give me a game when we're off someplace in Podunk with an afternoon to kill? And just between us, Charlie, I can teach 'em the business a hell of a lot quicker than I can teach 'em to really hit the ball."

The key phrase here is "give me a game," which means a game roughly in his class—not too bad, but not too impossibly good either. So watch your step.

How to Lose to Your Boss

This can be trickier than it sounds, because there's nothing more damaging than to have your boss think you're either trying to let him win or partronizing him tenniswise. In fact, the important consideration is not so much whether he wins or not, but *whether you make him look good and feel good.*

It's better even to beat him slightly, from time to time, in a close match, if you make him think that with you he plays the best tennis he's ever played. Play to his strength, especially if you can do it subtly. Say, for example, that you know he has a very nice backhand if the bounce isn't too high, or if it isn't too deep. You could murder him with a topspin lob to his backhand corner. So don't. Give him good, brisk but flat drives to his backhand, not too deep.

> *"Gosh, J.B., I kept pounding your backhand like the book says, but they all came sizzling back!"*
>
> *(He will give you an inscrutable smile. After all, if he got to be boss, he must have some basic animal cunning.)*
>
> *"That's right, boy, play the guy's weakness. You didn't pound it enough!"*

If he has a good forehand return of service, give him hard serves, not lollipops, right to the forehand, and make them flat, never twists that break into his body.

> *"There I was, J.B., slamming in my two-dollar serve, and what do I get back? Rockets!"*
>
> *"I was playin' way over my head today, boy. Must be this new racquet."*

Lots of middle-aged executives can hit the ball fairly well if they can get to it. The problem is legs. If you have a beautifully disguised drop shot that starts out looking like a drive and dies miserably just beyond the net, forget it. Save it for that ladder match at the club. Don't just pop them right to him either. Give him two or three brisk steps on every shot.

If it's really ridiculous, if you were the captain of the Yale tennis team, or something, and he's a rabbit who can't get beyond low C in his club, with no possible strengths to play to, he may really welcome some help, if you can give it to him tactfully.

> "With that great forehand of yours, J.B., you'd be a killer if we could beef up the backhand. Did you ever try a backswing like this? I'll hit you some." (If you could ever get him into class B, he'd probably make you a vice-president!)

Be His Doubles Partner

If he can't beat you, join him. Of, if his singles is almost impossible, make him your doubles partner. In fact, no matter what, try to make him your partner. It's even better than being his son-in-law. Many young doubles partners of yesterday are now captains of industry. Let him know you need his help.

> "You know, J.B., my weakness is strategy. With your brains and my brawn, we might even win the company doubles championship." (WARNING: this is a very tricky wicket if you aren't good enough to bring it off. Sometimes the only way for a boss to get rid of a losing partner is to send him off to that branch office in Mud Flats.)

But if you do get him to join you, always create the impression that he's making a real contribution, even if he misses every shot he takes.

> *"Spooky, isn't it, J.B., how much better I play when there's some sense of direction. You make me realize tennis isn't just a slam-bang thing!"*

Or,

> *"I guess what I've been needing all this time is a great quarterback, J.B."*

Even when you are truly magnificent, always remember the higher values.

> *"Great shot, boy!"*
> *"After the way you set it up, J.B., all I had to do was put it away."*

Opposite Number Doubles

If you really want to consolidate your position, try a little opposite-numbermanship. Watch for a young player at your club or in local tournaments who is in a similar strategic position in another company and is also cultivating executives. Then talk to your boss.

> *"Pal of mine is over at Blamco, J.B. His doubles partner is sort of a veep in charge of purchasing. I suggested we might have a doubles some lunch time."*
> *"And so it runs a little into the afternoon, eh, boy?"*

Soon you may develop client contacts of your own. Then no one will mind where you hold your discussions as long as they are fruitful. A few cool beers on the club terrace after a brisk game, and who knows what the cash-flow will be?

Beware of Rivals

Now that everyone is playing tennis, these ideas may occur to others. If one of your rivals in the company seems to have the idea of taking your place as the boss' doubles partner, try to prevent it. If there are four of you choosing up partners to play, jump in quickly to get your man.

> *"Shall we take them on, J.B.?"*

And if your rival suggests,

> *"It might be more even the other way,"*

then just say:

> *"Are you sure? I haven't played for ages."* (This is good because it indicates (1) that you're modest and magnanimous, and (2) that you're basically good, and certain in the end to be better. And add quickly: *"Why don't we just try one set this way and see how it goes."*)

During the game refer jokingly to the Good Guys (you and the boss) and the Bad Guys (them).

> *"Well, that's three to nothing* (better than "love" in this context) *for the Good Guys."*

And then, when you get back to your baseline together,

> *"Well, looks like the old team is invincible, J.B., right?"*

Try to force your opponents to make some easy returns; for instance, when you've driven your rival into his backhand corner with a well-placed forehand drive, he may have to poop up a weak, short lob. "Yours, J.B.!" you shout, and let him make the kill. "Great shot, J.B.!" Or, if he misses it in spite of everything: "Tough shot, J.B., he had a lot of nasty spin on it."

The Tennis-Playing Secretary and Her Role in Life

Most of the above devices, with variations, can be used by women junior executives. They can help a clever girl rise from secretaryship, too.

Remember that the girl who just sleeps with her boss can become his mistress or maybe even the head of women's personnel. But the girl who's his mixed-doubles partner can become the next Mrs. J.B., if that's what she's after. Or maybe a member of the Board of Directors.

This brings us to the whole massive subject of sex. Can tennis further your ends there, too? This subject is so complex it requires a chapter of its own.

16 / Sex and Club Tennis

The relationships between sex and club tennis can be both frightening and rewarding

SHOULD TENNIS PLAYERS GIVE UP SEX?

Are tennis and sex really counterproductive? Can sex destroy tennis? Can tennis bring you more sex? Well, yes, a guarded yes, to both questions.

Actually there are two opposing theories about the first question—whether sex is physically bad for tennis—which we'll call the Blonstein Theory and the Namath Theory. And since both have points to recommend them, you can choose the one you like.

The Blonstein Theory

Or don't, fellows. In fact, don't girls! Be a monk. Be virginal. It'll show up on the scoreboard.

This chilling and puritanical dictum has been sent down to all (and published officially by the British Lawn Tennis Association) by Dr. J. L. Blonstein, Hon. Medical Advisor to the British Olympic Team. Dr. B.'s stand is purely medical, not moral. Tennis players—in fact, *all* athletes—"ought to abstain completely even the week before." A whole week! The reason is a matter of adrenalin. "The body builds up a supply of adrenalin, which is converted into nor-adrenalin." And sex, Dr. B. says, can use this up, leaving the player, male or female, with less punch and pow.

I was worried about this, and interviewed a former high-ranking British tournament player on the subject. Could he give me anything specific on it? (For reasons that will become apparent, he shall have to be nameless here, but the case history is true.)

He said he could give me an excellent example. He and his doubles partner, whom we'll call Roger, were on a tennis trip to play a big tournament and were sharing the same hotel room. Roger, who was at the time engaged to a lovely girl, elsewhere at the moment, was admired greatly by the local young ladies and repeatedly asked my informant if he'd mind taking a walk or having a bit of practice so that the room might offer him a bit of scope. My friend tactfully complied, and there was rather continual activity of the sort that Dr. Blonstein felt would consume adrenalin, but without producing scores.

> *"Nothing you could do about it?" I asked.*
> *"Felt it was his personal problem, you know."*
> *"Pity, so you lost the doubles event?"*
> *"No, actually, we won, quite easily. Roger seemed frightfully relaxed. Bore the whole brunt, really. I was a bit edgy, you know."*

There's another story of a traveling British player, and the question of whether his wife should accompany him on a tennis tour.

"Actually," said the coach, "I rather favored it. Felt if she were along, he'd have less sexual activity."

This leads us to the second theory.

The Namath Theory

Joe Namath, probably the best known and perhaps the

best rewarded American football player, recommended sex almost as part of a training program. He felt that having a woman the night before a big game steadied his nerves and allowed him to concentrate entirely on football on the day of the game.

He often followed this advice himself, and it certainly worked for him.

For the club player there are at least two considerations. Which is more important—the extra one or two games or the, ah, quality of life?

And also, will it help or hurt your game? If you're the type who tends to be sluggish in a match and needs more pep and energy, then (if the match is important enough for such drastic measures) wait until afterward to celebrate or to console yourself.

On the other hand, if you're the jumpy type who never plays as well in an important match as you do in practice, then live it up. The Namath Theory may apply. It may steady your nerves, and your concentration may be disturbed less when that gorgeous redhead on the sidelines crosses her (or his) legs.

Determining whether you are a Blonstein or a Namath person should be a matter of careful individual study. Keep accurate records.

"Wednesday night, Peg; Thursday night, Janie; Friday night, Lulu; Saturday afternoon, beat Joe in ladder match. 6–3, 7–5. Relaxed, confident, not unduly bothered by having Madge on sidelines in bikini."

(Following week) "Wednesday, Thursday, Friday, couldn't get a date anywhere. Saturday, lost ladder match to Joe, 3–6, 5–7. Bit jumpy, no concentration. Madge there again in bikini, had lovely evening with her."

On the basis of this information you could prepare graphs showing your sex-tennis profile. It could be a guide to your subsequent behavior, and might even be a step in the march of science.

TENNIS AS A SEX-GATHERING TOOL

Once you've determined whether or not sex hurts your tennis, you may ask yourself, "Does tennis help me sexually?" There is little or no experimental evidence proving it will help your sexual performance. Undoubtedly it will keep you in better condition and give you better muscular tone and a trimmer, sexier body. However this may be counterbalanced by the fact that after half a dozen hard sets you have the problem of staying awake.

However it's clear that a tennis club will give you greater sexual opportunities whether you're male or female, if only because on weekends or summer evenings, it's where everybody *is*.

But remember that a tennis club, sexually speaking, is a psychological jungle, with tensions and conflicts almost more than some people can bear. This doesn't mean that they are always unpleasant. They can even be titillating, with overtones that border on the erotic. Note these curious factors:

Item: Tennis is one of the few sports in which men and women play in adversary positions, in face-to-face conflict. Every tennis match is in a real sense a fight, a duel, the object being to inflict a kind of ritual destruction, and domination of the other, during which projectiles are aggressively driven at each other at considerable speed. It is a game in which a skillful woman can, and often does, thoroughly thrash and even humiliate a man who is larger and stronger than herself, and in full view of his friends, both male and female.

Words like whip, beat, crush, murder, and massacre are often heard at tennis clubs, although no one is trying to inflict physical pain, nor is a drop of blood ever spilled, except, perhaps, from an occasional skinned knee. Though you may hear "She massacred him!" or "She murdered him, and sent him home crying!" in actual fact no skin was even broken and few if any tears shed. They may even have had a couple of beers together afterward and then left-arm-in-arm for his place.

Item: Both love-making and tennis are mind-bending combinations of the mental and the physical; in both cases, psychological factors are as important, if not more important, than the physical. We all know that the physical skills of love-making are relatively simple compared with a really good all-court game and take far less time to acquire. The skills are not interchangeable; one can be extremely proficient at one of them and ludicrously bad at the other. And of course the physical attributes (size, body shape, etc.) of the best tennis player may differ markedly from the upper reaches of the wow-index or id-quotient, though we can all think of examples in which both sets of superlatives are gloriously present. But how many Gussie Morans are there? Or, girls, how many Borgs or Panattas?

Item: In tennis alone, the ideal doubles partner may be quite different from the ideal tennis opponent or the ideal sexual partner. You can see that we already have three different people or consorts.

For example, one of my favorite mixed-doubles partners was a charming lady who might be described as the poor man's Chris Evert. She preferred the back court and would come to the net only if carried. She never missed a ground shot, and could hit lovely drives all day off both sides and into both corners. And she could run like a rabbit. I could charge boyishly to the net to volley and smash and know that anything that went past me would be dealt with efficiently. As doubles partners we were blissfully happy. You might say that mixed-doubles-wise we were madly in love. Yet as an opponent she'd have driven me crazy, passing me neatly every time I went to the net. And as a sexual partner we'd have been geometrically ridiculous, since she was about half my size.

Item: In all clubs there are two major types of females: tennis girls and after-tennis girls, and seldom do the twain meet. The after-tennis girl is easy to spot. She's just had a fancy hair-do, and she wouldn't muss it up for anything. Well, she might for anything, but not for tennis. She may be in tennis clothes, but not the kind you can actually *play* in, and she may be wearing ear-rings, or even a necklace, and bracelets. She performs almost entirely on the terrace and in the club bar. She looks like a queen compared with the soaking wet, pony-tailed, red-faced, court-stained wenches who come dragging in from the wars.

ARE THERE AFTER-TENNIS MEN, TOO?

Indeed there are. You'll find them, girls, not so much by looking at their clothes or their coiffures as by, well, a bitter-sweet lopsided smile across a crowded room, which shows you that they have placed a, well, higher value on things. They *do* play, and by the way they play you can tell that they have a wider range of interests than tennis alone. To them tennis isn't everything, and they are certainly not everything to tennis. It is a matter of emphasis, of philosophy, and the fact that they recently, perhaps that very day, may have been splattered against the wall by some frightful little person who overemphasizes the game.

In short, girls, they believe in moderation in all things, especially tennis, and they may even have something left for you later in the evening.

HOW WOMEN CAN HELP MALE TENNIS PLAYERS

Some women want to be the club champion, and that's just a matter of good coaching and reading some of those books that tell you which grip to use.

However, the true tenniswoman will really be seeking somewhat more than that. She'll have a higher purpose. She will see a tennis club as a place where she can help others and, of course, help herself. The place will be crowded with males, at times when males are allowed outdoors, and if you're the right kind of woman, you'll want to know how you can do them the most good.

At the end of every tennis day you'll find men limping around the club, licking their psychological wounds. They will need you.

First you'll have to decide: should you be a tennis girl or an after-tennis girl? Be the latter only if you are totally hopeless at tennis and can't hit the ball over the net. In this case your mission will be to show the wounded male players that tennis isn't everything and that life goes on.

It's far better to be a dual-purpose girl. The purely decorative female is regarded by male tennis players as just another pretty face. And since he won't be seeing your name on the tournament draw-sheets or the court-reservation board, he may not even know what it is. You will be nothing but another sexual object.

The dual-purpose tennis-and-after girl is the one he'll marry or make into his business partner, whichever you prefer. The trick is to run into the showers immediately after the game and snake up. Come out fragrant, tanned, blooming, and eager.

Another thing to remember is that the quickest way to a tennis player's heart is something long and cool and wet after he's come off the court. It doesn't even have to be alcoholic, though that won't hurt. Everybody loses a couple of quarts of moisture out there on a warm day. Any normal male would prefer a frosty quart of something wet to Raquel Welch or even you. That is, he'd want the drink first. Get a reputation for mint juleps or gin slings or even the best iced tea in town, and you'll have the men where you want them—at your place.

It's also good to remember that a strong arm isn't everything and that the tennis ladder isn't always as important as the parking lot ladder or what he does in his spare time; i.e., when he's not playing. Don't be afraid of the man who lets his business interfere occasionally with his tennis.

> *"Oh, honey, Phil was looking for you. I think he wants you for a partner in the mixed."*
> *"Which one is Phil?"*
> *"He's the one with the beautiful smash."*

Of course, if that's what you're looking for—a beautiful smash—go right ahead.

> *"Which is the one who owns the Porsche?"*
> *"That's Gerald. He's really not very good. He's that slightly plump one who went to Harvard Business School."*

"Does he play mixed?"

Remember, it's always possible to improve his game.

SHOULD I BEAT HIM?

If you beat him, make it seem that *he has shown you how to beat him* and you're terribly grateful.

> *"You should never have told me that bit about the backhand, Gerald. It does make such a difference."*
> *"You certainly caught on fast, pet."*
> *"Explain the theory of it to me again."*

Beat him only about one time in three at first. You might look back to the part in the previous chapter about how to lose to your boss, because the same general principles apply. Hit to his strength, hard, and make him feel that you bring out the best in him. At first, until you've trained him up a bit, don't hit them too far out of his reach. Make sure he gets to most of them.

HOW TO PLAY WITH YOUR HUSBAND

Once you've married him, it's all right to give him a good, hard beating once in a while. Really knock him around and make him run back and forth. Most men don't get enough exercise, and it will improve his motivations and make him practice more.

Remember that wherever you hit the ball, he will have to run there to get it. It may be the only time in your married life when you can make him do exactly what you want him to do.

> *"Very good, Gerald, you're running like a deer."*
> *"Really, like a deer?"*
> *"Yes, dear. And it's so good for you."*

It is even possible to run him back and forth mercilessly and still let him win as many points as you like. It will do wonders for his figure, and everyone will notice it.

> *"My dear, you don't seem to have a hair out of place, and look at poor Gerald! Do you make him run behind your car?"*
> *"It's because he's so athletic. He always pulverizes me. Don't you, Gerald? Gerald!"*

If you've chosen the right man, you should have some help in the house. This will give you more time to play, and you'll improve faster than he does. Make it up to him by being his doubles partner.

> *"Young Butch wants me to play with him in the open mixed, Gerald. We have a good chance to win it. But I'll play with you in the handicap. John said if I played with you, he'd give us lots of points every game."*

Generally speaking, though, a woman doesn't need to be too good to get the most out of club play. The girl who can beat and does beat most of the men in the club isn't likely to be too popular with them.

You'll get down to the question, which is more important, tennis or anything? The best position for anything is to be slightly above the middle of the women's ladder, perhaps a high B, with a good doubles game, which means that you can volley well. Then you'll be asked to play a lot of mixed doubles, and that's the way to get to know everybody.

HOW TO BE A BOMBSHELL

It's always possible to go all out for pure sensation and be the most talked-about player in the club, even if you're not the best one.

Though men aren't entirely ruled out of this category, so far the historic bombshells have all been ladies, and they have done it with clothes. Or it was done *to* them, and often by that stop-at-nothing tennis-togs designer, Teddy Tinling. His main weapon was panties, but you don't have to stop there. Tinling had to stop there, because the players are always inspected at Wimbledon before they go out on court—just to guard against things like this—and T-T counted on that ingrained British reserve not to look *under* the skirt, and the panties, discreetly hidden from the inspector, were not unfurled until it was too late, and the players were in violent action on the court.

Tinling's two great shockers, which made him immortal, were Gussie Moran's (lace) and Maria Bueno's (shocking pink) panties. There was another, perhaps even bolder attempt made on behalf of beautiful Karol Fageros (gold lamé), which was blocked by the security forces in time to avoid arousing naked emotions on the hallowed turf.

Did it work? Well, Gussie was really gorgeous (probably still is), and the panties were just the icing (if that's the word) on the cheesecake. But her sensational panties got her a fat contract with the pros.

Maria didn't need to wear controversial panties. She

had all the glory anyway, winning all the major championships and playing the most beautiful and graceful tennis I've ever seen. She was like a ballerina. But I won't forget that day of the flaming derrière, and the 17,000 *ooooooh's* in Wimbledon's center court every time Maria stretched for a low shot. We were happy to see her again after a long absence from the game in the 1976 Wimbledon. No pink panties, but the same grace and skill. Amazingly she reached the fourth round, in spite of her years of illness.

So, how badly do you want bombshell glory at your club? As far as I know, nobody's yet tried mink or rhinestone panties, and the whole topless field is, you might say, wide open.

I know of no male who's gone for sheer sex appeal in the clothes department. The two most recent teeny-bopper swoon builders, Panatta and Borg, broke no hearts because of what they *wore*. Arthur Ashe really broke the ice on tennis whites by wearing yellow (colors still are not allowed at Wimbledon), and Don Budge was famous for his impeccable white flannels. I'll never understand how anyone managed long woolen trousers when the temperature at the Forest Hills bake-oven stadium hit 95° Fahrenheit!

The field is wide open, though, for some publicity-seeker in a Tarzan leopard skin, a predominantly white leopard skin for Wimbledon, and maybe bare-bottomed photos on an astro-turf rug.

DON'T SPIN OFF YOUR GIRL FRIENDS

As a male, you too can reap a rich harvest at your tennis club, which will be full of girls, many of them there actually to play tennis.

Be careful, however. You can mix tennis and sex, but it's complicated and sometimes difficult.

Let's say you've found a girl who is shaped the way you think all girls should be, and has a pretty smile and a twinkle in her eyes. And then, wonder of wonders, you're thrown together in a brisk mixed doubles, and you find that she's no pitty-patter. She hits a solid, hard drive off both sides and even dares to charge the net and volley. All this, and she's sexy, too. You have found the dream woman. You are in tennis-love, a most dangerous condition. You have a cool drink together after the doubles.

> "*Maybe we could knock around a few together some day?*"
>
> "*Oh, you mean singles?*" (*She still looks gorgeous in spite of the fact that she's as wet and bedraggled as you are.*) "*I don't think I could give you a game!*"
>
> "*The way you were playing today you'd probably massacre me.*" (*You almost believe it.*)

So you make a date, and arrive on the court in that fancy pair of English shorts you always save for the club tournament. You're pleased to note that she's wearing a low-cut tennis dress that fits her like a bathing suit, and a new hair ribbon to match the dingus on her dress. She's trying to please you, bless her little heart.

You know that concentration, on tennis that is, is going to be difficult, and you know she mustn't beat you too easily. No woman respects a man she can humiliate. You must try to beat her, by a whisker, and then maybe you can have a nice dinner, and who knows what?

You let her serve first, with her back to the sun. Give her every advantage. Her serve comes in nicely—hard, flat ones to your backhand corner. She makes the first two points. You go into your most aggressive receiving crouch and got a point, but she still goes to 40–15 and game.

You're worried. She bats back your first two serves for winners. You lean on the next one and net it. Your usually reliable second serve, a twist, not very hard, works, and she plops it into the net. At 15–30 you try the twist as a first serve, hitting harder, and she misses it altogether. Back in the deuce court you do a slice serve that kicks to the outside, and she misses that too. A twist serve to the advantage court gives you the game.

She serves to your backhand again, and you just reach it with a desperate slice, cut very hard. She nets it. You hit a hard, flat forehand on the next serve, come in, and she passes you. You hit a heavy topspin on the next one, and she nets it.

What's happening? You're losing almost every point on flat balls and almost always winning on the spins. Assuming you're an idiot and haven't realized this, you carry on and win the set easily, 6–1. She says she wants to stop because she isn't feeling well. And the next time you call her, she says she has a date.

You've spun her away. Like most women, even some pretty good players—and especially if they play mostly with other women—she is put off by spin, doesn't like it, and even feels it's somehow not sportsmanlike.

I don't know why this is true. Women can certainly learn to use spin as well as men. Rosie Casals has one of the hardest-kicking twist serves in the business. Chris Evert uses heavy topspin, and so on. Almost all the top tournament girls use lots of educated spin and use it well. But most women club players don't. If you want to put that uppity girl in her place, use spin. But if you're interested in other kinds of conquest, hit the balls nice and flat and go easy on the drop shots. Be careful of smashes, too. Women fear them, with reason. If you must smash, aim well away from them. Offensively, women tend to be

weak here, though I've known a few who could knock off
your ears.

HOW TO USE TENNIS TO END AFFAIRS

Since naked emotions are always so close to the surface in
tennis players, they can easily be brought out and put to
use in practical ways. Tennis can be used as a lure, almost
as an aphrodisiac, but can also be used by skilled opera-
tors of both sexes to bring a quick conclusion to something that at least one of you feels has gone on for too
long. You can use tennis to make a clean, quick break.

Case History No. 1

Lulu A., while having a close personal relationship with
Ralph B., often played singles with him and kept the
scores even by placing balls where he could reach them.
The day after hearing that Ralph was also carrying on a
relationship with Yvonne C., Lulu kept the ball just out of
his reach, beat him 6–0, 6–0, and walked off the court
without a word.

Case History No. 2

Wilmer D., who was keeping company with Ellen E.,
had never told her that he was, secretly, a Jekyll-and-Hyde
tennis player. As a young man playing in Hackensack,
New Jersey, he had been a chopper and in fact was
known as the Abominable Hackenchopper. He always
won the club's class B tournament, but was hated by everyone.

Seeking love, a new existence, and somebody who

would play tennis with him, he changed his tennis life entirely by taking lessons and getting rid of his chopper habits. He left New Jersey (his job was in New York City) and moved to Long Island, revealing his move to no one. And since it is easier on a weekend to go from New York to Denver than from New Jersey to Long Island, no one at his new club ever learned the truth. He never again played anything but nice tennis, and he gained friends and the very close relationship with Ellen E. He had a firm place in the middle of the C class in the club ladder.

However, Wilmer desired, for complicated reasons, to end his relationship with Ellen. (One of the reasons was a stunning new blonde club member.) He took Ellen onto a back court at a time when no one was around, threw off his mask, figuratively speaking, and became Wilmer the Abominable Hackenchopper. Though they had previously played evenly, this time Ellen was unable to hit a single ball for five games, and when they changed courts for the sixth, she slapped his face and ran straight to the showers and out of his life altogether.

Though Wilmer was not proud of the episode, he felt he had done what he had to do, and he never again chopped a ball. Ellen later married and had five children. She and her husband play golf.

SHOULD I PLAY TENNIS WITH MY WIFE?

This resolves itself into several other questions, such as, Which came first, the tennis or the wife? Should you marry your mixed-doubles partner? Should you make your wife into your mixed-doubles partner? The answer to the second and third questions is, of course, "No!"

If the tennis came first, and you're marrying her because she's the perfect mixed-doubles partner, then beware! It is far easier to find a compatible wife than a really good doubles partner, and if you marry your partner, you are bound to destroy the smooth, harmonious relationship that made you so successful together on the court. All sorts of trivial matters, i.e., those totally unrelated to tennis, are sure to come up.

> *"Stand back a bit for his first serve, pet, and watch the twist."*
>
> *"Right. Did you remember to turn off the oven?"*
>
> *"I distinctly told you to do that, pet, and—"*

You see it's impossible.

If the marriage came first, trying to hone her carefully into the perfect mixed-doubles partner is certain to wreck it.

> *"I know what you're thinking, George."*
>
> *"I wasn't thinking. I was just chewing my beans."*
>
> *"You're thinking if I hadn't missed that volley on match point, then—"*
>
> *"No, no, hon, not at all!"*
>
> *"I think we should bring these things out into the open, George. Is it too painful to talk about?"*

Maybe it is.

If she weren't your wife, the whole tragic episode would be forgotten by the next weekend, and you'd be ready for the next match.

On the other hand, if the only possible way of holding onto the perfect partner is to marry her, then you may have to bow to the inevitable. So marry her, and then be prepared for the pitfalls.

TENNIS ADULTERY AND HOW TO
LIVE WITH IT

These are strong words, but strange things are happening now that everyone, including your boss, is playing tennis.

Suppose you have that ultimate, almost unobtainable combination, the perfect wife and the perfect doubles partner rolled into one. You know she is an absolutely faithful, loving wife. She wouldn't think of sleeping with anyone else. But your boss, who may be married (for the second or third time) to Miss Piston Rings of 1972, needs a good tennis partner.

> *"Davie, J.B. asked me if I'd play with him in the company mixed."*
>
> *"But you're playing with me! We ought to win it!"*
>
> *"I told him yes, Davie. I mean he did play for Harvard, back before the flood. Do you want me to tell him you won't let me?"*

She's got you and she knows it. This can lead to all kinds of things.

> *"Damn! J.B. is sending me to Seattle on Friday!"*
>
> *"Should be wonderful for you company-wise."*
>
> *"He wants you for the Eastern State mixed on Saturday."*
>
> *"Jimmy did suggest that, dear."*
>
> *"Jimmy?"*
>
> *"J.B., darling. He does have the cutest topspin lob! We were going to dinner afterward."*
>
> *"To dinner? You and J.B.?"*
>
> *"The three of us, darling. Linda's coming, too— probably in gold lamé with an opal in her navel.*

You don't have to worry about that part, Lover.
Jimmy says I'm his outdoor girl."
    "Seattle, here I come!"

It may be great for you at the company. Try to find another girl—for tennis, that is. A *younger* girl, with a nice drop volley. But not with an opal in her navel.

SHOULD I PLAY AGAINST MY WIFE?

Never, if you can avoid it.

In the first place, everyone in the club will think automatically that no one else will play with you. Men play with their wives when no one else will play with them.

Practice with your wife, never play with her. Practicing is good because it's helpful and friendly. Playing is bad because it makes you her enemy. She will think you are trying to defeat and destroy her. Either that, or you are trying *not* to defeat her, which is even worse.

> *"I don't mind if you beat me, Harold, as long as*
> *you do it* nicely."
>   *"Do you mind if I lose to you nicely?"*
>   *"If you're going to talk like that, I'm going to go*
> *home."*

In fact, some men and women refuse to play with any member of the opposite sex. "Never," they say, "mix sex and tennis!" And who is to say they're wrong?

Appendix
The Language of Tennis

Or which came first, the racket or the balls?

Since tennis is one of the world's oldest games, and since its origins are both French and English, its language can be traced far, far back into the history and language of both these countries. The original center of tennis gravity was France, but it shifted centuries later to England.

The origin of the word *tennis* is most likely the French word *tenez* from the verb *tenir*. The server supposedly shouted Tenez! when he served, meaning Attention! or Take that! (since the verb *tenir* means almost everything) or our Ready? This origin goes way back. One early account states that French knights introduced the game in Florence in 1325. How long before that it was played, I don't know.

Tennis was the English word *tenys* in 1460, which rhymed with pennies. (Today of course it rhymes with dollars, which rhymes with hollers, as in Team Tennis.) It also has been spelled *tennys* (1463), *tenyce* (1470), and *tennes* (1525).

Henry VIII played it at Hampdon Court in a court-yard. The original "real" tennis court or "court" tennis court is still there, a weird combination of walls and roofs and windows. (During the Queens Club tournament in London, tea is usually served in one of these courts.) Tennis was evidently a kind of royal prerogative forbidden to common folk, like shooting deer, because there's mention of "tenys, or other unlawful games." Henry preferred his subjects to practice archery for national defense. And for those who thought that *tenys*, like *detente*, was a wicked foreign word, it was sometimes called *tosse the ball*.

Tennis wasn't always played in palace courtyards. In 1793, *Sporting Magazine* said that "field tennis threatens ere long to bowl out cricket." It hasn't done it yet, though.

SPHAIRISTIKE, ANYONE?

But tennis didn't really get going until one day in 1873, when some Englishmen were gazing at a pretty croquet lawn.

> *"Wouldn't it be nice to play Sphairistike here?"*
> *"I beg your pardon?"*
> *"Sphairistike, old boy. Greek for 'play ball!' you know. One plays it with a racket, a ball, and a net. We could mark out a court right here on the grass."*

And they did. The court was shaped somewhat like an hour-glass, narrower at the net. The game caught on.

> *"Sphairistike, anyone?"*
> *"Oh, yes, ra-*ther, *Fraffly good game! How do you spell it?"*
> *"Haven't the foggiest. Just play it, you know."*

They decided, thank goodness, to go back to the old word *tennis*, but to avoid confusion with the courtyard game, they called their game *lawn tennis*. They really did play it on a lawn. They straightened out the hour-glass shape, and wrote up a set of rules which were almost exactly the same as those used today. The first Wimbledon was held, and actually at Wimbledon, in 1877.

IS *RACQUET* REALLY THE CQUEEN'S ENGLISH?

And which came first, the racket or the balls?

When is a racquet a racket? Well, in an indoor court, a racquet certainly makes a racket. But is *racquet* right? Is that really the Cqueen's English, like *cheque* for check? Or is *racket* American? Well, *raquette* is French. Where on earth did that redundant "c" cquome from anyway?

Racket is *not* an Americanization, as you might think. Shakespeare spelled it that way. And which *did* come first, the racket or the balls? Well, the racket did, because when *racket* was used, in 1603, there were no balls, only balles, and the French *still* have balles.

Obviously, old rackets made more racket than racquets do now, because then they were both the same word, *racket,* which is onomatopoetic. Shakespeare made a pun about that and the Tennis Court Keeper in *Henry IV*.

Just a few years ago, the American spelling fashion in most books about tennis was *racket,* and it still is in England, where *Tennis* magazine spells it *racket.* Recently, fickle American spelling went over to *racquet,* which I've used in this book.

I do prefer splitting the two words, keeping *racket* as a loud noise or commotion and as something the Mafia has, and *racquet* for tennis, so that racketeers are different from racqueteers. If we had to be brash simple-spelling Americans, we could drop the useless *c* to make *raquet,* which goes with *thru* and *tho* and *tonite,* and we could then refer to a tennis match as a *raquet-fite.* Or, to go along with the Aussies' Qantas, we could make it *raqet,* and delight (delite?) Scrabble players everywhere.

DOES LOVE MEAN NOTHING TO THE ENGLISH?

It should be no surprise that *love* comes from the French, but the French are forever puzzled that *love* to the English and the Americans is a synonym for nothing. They feel it may have something to do with our way of life.

In fact, in my early days of trying to play tennis in French, I confused my opponent, a lovely French-speaking Swiss girl when I announced scores.

> *"Amour–trente." (Or as I thought, Love–thirty. She looked pleased, but puzzled.)*
> *"Merci, mon trésor* [or *thanks, sweetie-pie*]—*but what is the score?"*
> *"Amour–trente."*
> *"The tennis court is no place for that."*

She explained to me that the French have always thought that love is not nothing, that it is really something. The French never use *amour* for nothing, only *zero,* or *rien,* which means nothing. Long ago, however, the French used *the egg* or *l'oeuf* for zero, as we sometimes use a *great big goose egg* for zero. The English quickly corrupted *l'oeuf* to *love,* and thus *love* came to mean zero.

In keeping score the French say nothing for nothing if the server is ahead, just *trente,* or thirty, instead of thirty–love. Only if the receiver is ahead do they say *zero–trente*, or love–thirty. Makes sense, doesn't it?

Let's continue with French scoring as long as we're on the subject and approaching deuce. After 30–40, if the score is equal, the French usually use *quarante–partout* (forty–everywhere), or forty–all. Only after 40–40 do they use *égalité*, or deuce. And to confuse the scoring still further, they sometimes use *égalité* to mean any equal score, like "égalité–quinze à" or "deuce–fifteen all."

A THUMBNAIL GLOSSARY FOR THE INTERNATIONAL TENNIS BUM

Really good tennis players never stay home. They go flapping all over the world. So if you get good and go for the Grand Slam (Forest Hill, Wimbledon, Paris, Australia), you'll need a few extra words.

Ad, Van, and Advantage. When its your advantage, Americans use *Your ad* and the English use *Your van*, pronounced "van," and not "vawn" (though they do say "ad-vawn-tage"). The French always use the whole word—*avantage*.

Alleys. To Americans those strips you use only in doubles are alleys. The English call them tram lines, because they do look like street car tracks, don't they? They're corridors or *couloirs* to the French.

Five. Americans use *five* as a lazy abbreviation of fifteen, as in five–forty. The English understand what *five* means, and even say it once in a while. Because *quinze* is just as easy to say as *cinq*, the French always use *quinze*.

Tie-Breaker. The tie-breaker is an American invention, but it is now an international word, though often, as in France, shortened to *tie-break.*

Not-up. Not-up is the American umpire's cry for a double bounce. The English understand what it means, but they are more likely to use *double bounce.*

F.B.I. The English are sometimes startled when an American asks "F.B.I.?" before the first serve of the game. The correct answer is "No, I'm C.I.A.," but "Yes" or "No." Of course he's asking "First ball in?" The custom is common in both France and England for friendly matches, too, but never in serious tournaments.

Two-and-one, etc. This abbreviated form of scoring takes sixes for granted. Thus, beating someone two-and-one means that you won 6–2, 6–1. This scoring is less common, but understood in England. It's especially convenient when reporting scores at the referee's stand.

Index

About the Author

Shepherd Mead, the author of many books, is perhaps best known for *How to Succeed in Business Without Really Trying.* When he's not writing books, Mead is likely to be playing tennis or else watching the experts at Wimbledon or Forest Hills.